KALEIDOSCOPE

LOTHIAN

Edited by Simon Harwin

First published in Great Britain in 1999 by
POETRY NOW YOUNG WRITERS
Remus House, Coltsfoot Drive,
Woodston, Peterborough, PE2 9JX
Telephone (01733) 890066

HB ISBN 0 75430 417 5
SB ISBN 0 75430 418 3

FOREWORD

This year, the Poetry Now Young Writers' Kaleidoscope competition proudly presents the best poetic contributions from over 32,000 up-and-coming writers nationwide.

Successful in continuing our aim of promoting writing and creativity in children, each regional anthology displays the inventive and original writing talents of 11-18 year old poets. Imaginative, thoughtful, often humorous, *Kaleidoscope Lothian* provides a captivating insight into the issues and opinions important to today's young generation.

The task of editing inevitably proved challenging, but was nevertheless enjoyable thanks to the quality of entries received. The thought, effort and hard work put into each poem impressed and inspired us all. We hope you are as pleased as we are with the final result and that you continue to enjoy *Kaleidoscope Lothian* for years to come.

CONTENTS

Fettes College

Eilidh Hall	62
Rebecca Hitchen	62
Hannah Clarke	63
Melvin Byres	64
Camilla McCorkell	65
Emma-Kate Hunter	66
Denis Zoubkov	67
Fiona Mould	68
Cornelius Dirkzwager	69
Tamsin Murley	70

George Heriot's School

Ivor Williams	70
Neave Corcoran	71
Simon Donne	72
Peter Black	72
Elizabeth Welsh	73
Christian McDermott	74
Ruth H Siller	74
Philip Williams	75
Fiona MacCuish	76
Alistair Scott	77
Vivienne Li	77
Laura Good	78
James Corcoran	79
Katharine Fox	80
Naomi Maxwell	81
Jane B M Crawford	82
Siobhan M Ogilvie	83
Jackie Ritchie	84
Paul McNally	85
Nicholas I Johnston	86
Amie Barr	86
Graeme Hawkins	87
Richard Mason	87
Scott Cable	88
David Jung	88

Grant Wilson	89
Cara Neish Millar	90

James Gillespie's High School

Christopher Hoban	90
Chris Kelly	91
Rachel Newton	91
Paul Connolly	92
Saadia Shad	92
Elaine Cunningham	93
Katharine Greig	93
Katie McAra	94
Sheryl Balloch	94
Fiona Rutherford	95
Sonya S Mansoor	96

Knox Academy

Neil Watt	96
Elinor Douse	97
Ellen Raine Leaver	98
Kirsty Bisset	99
Ross Blair	100
Colin Wood	100
Carrie McDonald	101
Gillian Welsh	102
Jennifer Caldwell	103
Gordon Drummond	104
Colin Fairgrieve	104
David Thomson	105
Wendy Rees	106
James Walker	106
Amanda Davidson	107
Graham Stewart	108
Laura Barrack	109
Naomi Cassells	110
Zoe Harris	110
Eilidh Imrie	111
Daniel Brunton	112

North Berwick High School

Penicuik High School

The Poems

TEACHERS

Oh we don't know but we've been told,
The teachers here are so old,
They help us with our work all day,
And then they let us out to play.
We think they are so smart and quick,
Their brains must be so big and thick.
They give us such a pile of tasks
And then sit and drink coffee from their flasks.
After school when we go home,
The teachers stay here all alone.
There's tons of work that's really bad,
To be a teacher you must be mad.

Steven Scott (11)
Blackford Brae Project

A WOOD IN AUTUMN

The woods in autumn are covered
In a flame of primrose crimson
This is the time for the jade-green leaves
To lose their colour to the powerful oncoming winter.
A fire of ochre and copper fall at my feet
The rustling leaves cause a russet-coloured
Squirrel to stop dead
For a moment I see its hazel markings
Then it's off
I'm alone in the woods now
Set alight by autumn
Giving way to the cold, harsh winter.

Alana C Currie (13)
Bo'ness Academy

THE REAL ME

Friends, dear friends,
What do you think,
Do you see personality,
Or do my qualities stink?

I like to go out and have a good laugh,
To see what's on sale,
And spend all my cash.

I hope to give laughter, comfort and joy,
To stick by you all no matter the cost,
And never to dump you like last Christmas' toy.

In school I do my best and give it my all,
I used to be called names because I did well,
You all experienced this and helped me grow tall,
No matter the situation you lot helped
If I ever did fall.

We all learn together and I respect you as mates,
And you gave me advice on my very first dates.

I'll never judge you or make you feel small,
I hope that you know I'll be there when you call.

I like to take part in gymnastics and play the piano,
To help others learn and tell them what I know.

I hope that we'll be together when we're all rickety and old,
And we'll gather together our pasts once retold.

So hear me dear friends,
Have your views of me changed,
One day I will leave you,
Your lives, rearranged.

Lauren Gray (14)
Bo'ness Academy

MY CRABBIT LITTLE SISTER

My crabbit little sister is so annoying,
She sits in the room all day drawing.
She couldn't even look after her hair,
So she got it chopped off, but said it wasn't fair.
When she is annoying I tell her to get lost,
But she goes away and acts as if she's the boss.
There must be something wrong with her brain,
Because she can't even spell her own name.
We all get peace when she goes away,
When she comes back we all run away.
She thinks that she is the best,
But I tell her she's nothing but a pest.

Hadia Ali (13)
Bo'ness Academy

SCHOOL

We go to school every day
All time for work and no time for play
When the bell goes at two minutes to nine
We stand outside class in a neat single line
When the bell goes at a quarter to four
There is a mighty roar as we rush to the door
The teacher shouts 'Homework'
We all moan and groan
Then she says 'Forget it, off you go home.'

Brian Donaldson (12)
Bo'ness Academy

FAMILY SECRETS

My mum is great she has a laugh,
She loves to soak in a bath.
Her smile disappears when I leave a mess,
She says, 'You cause me lots of stress!'

My dad's laid back but businesslike,
If I'm good I've hit a strike.
He loves to write and often reads,
And likes to make sure he succeeds.

My brother Owen is a big pain,
Sometimes he acts like he hasn't a brain.
He leaves a tip but he doesn't care,
Now he's gone the house is bare.

This is my family but they're nothing like me,
I am perfect I'm sure you'll agree.
I hope this poem has explained to you well,
All the facts I'm not supposed to tell!

Rona Shave (13)
Bo'ness Academy

SUDDEN DEATH

Suddenly fallen asleep in a foreign country,
Peacefully lying there with no pain,
Quiet surroundings with nothing but the sobbing of family,
No movement, looking so calm.
Me, sitting there knowing that I will never see a face
as cheery as yours again.

All the family back home, crying and depressed at the thought
of you alone,
Different people, different surroundings.
You lying there peacefully and cold but always watching over us.

Kirsty Samson (15)
Bo'ness Academy

LIVING UNDER ONE ROOF
(MY MUM)

Living with my mum
Sometimes isn't fun
She often drives me crazy
Telling me I'm lazy
But I love my mum . . .

         'Your room's a mess' she nags
         So I trudge upstairs with some black bags
         I switch on the telly
         And my room, who gives a nelly
         But I love my mum . . .

She always thinks she's right
So I shout at her with all my might
When she tries to be cool
She ends up looking like a fool
But I love my mum . . .

         But don't get me wrong
         We sometimes get along
         She always cooks and cleans
         Though I hate her baked beans
         But I love my mum.

Sarah Learmonth (13)
Bo'ness Academy

THE TRAIN JOURNEY

From my window I can see,
Lots of trees and a load of shrubs,
Rushing past as though they were moving,
All the steam rising up then disappearing
Lots of animals
Cows and sheep are just a few
Then we stopped at Aviemore,
'All aboard' someone said,
And we were off again.

Chugging along the rickety track,
Past all towns and villages too,
Oh I love the train, I do,
'On to Inverness' I say,
Train moving as fast as could be
Then we were there
Inverness, oh what a wonderful place.

Jonathan Birch (13)
Bo'ness Academy

LOVE

It is fast
It is slow
It makes the tears flow
It is there
but . . .
          you can't see it
but . . .
          I can feel it.

Graham Avery (12)
Bo'ness Academy

I Had An Accident

I had an accident
I ended up in hospital
I was in a ward with older people
I felt,
        Out of place
My mother was my only visitor
I was sad
None of my family visited me
I
  was
      rejected
  and
      dejected.
'Get well soon' arrived.

They thought of me and
That's what matters.

Michael McBain (13)
Bo'ness Academy

My Love

My love
      was a hundred miles away
so I rang him
      on his birthday.
This cost me half my pay
      I couldn't think of
         what to say.

Tiela Grant (12)
Bo'ness Academy

LIVING UNDER ONE ROOF
(MY MUM)

Living under the same roof as my mum
You'd think is bad.
But it's not bad, it's rather cool,
Even though she's quite mad.

My mum can be a pain sometimes,
When she's shouting at me.
But when she shouts a little too much,
She has a cup of tea.

My mum is really nice to me,
She buys me lots of stuff.
But she won't buy me anything,
When she thinks I've got enough.

I love my mum, I really do,
I'd be lost without her.
I'll always be right by her side,
Forever and ever.

Lyndsey Thomson (13)
Bo'ness Academy

WHY A LITTLE BROTHER

I wanted a little sister,
A little girl it would be,
But instead I got Graham,
A little boy you see.

Now I play at football,
And all these other games,
Most of the time I beat him,
And when I do he's a pain.

I'm glad I got a brother,
No Barbies in the house,
When he plays with Action Man,
He's as quiet as a mouse.

Kenneth Johnston (13)
Bo'ness Academy

MY BROTHER - THE PAIN

My brother and I get on very well,
But if he hits me, I won't ever tell,
He loves to write,
And start a fight,
When he's feeling reasonably happy.

My brother is nothing like my sister,
If she wakes up early she is crabbit,
Now she's had it,
My brother laughs,
When he's feeling reasonably happy.

If she can't think of a sentence to write,
She thinks about starting a stupid fight,
If she starts it,
She's in trouble,
My brother tells her that it's her homework,
If he's feeling reasonably happy.

I guess she isn't as bad as I think,
But is a pain,
But even though she can be annoying,
She still is kind
If she's feeling reasonably happy.

Sadia Ali (13)
Bo'ness Academy

MY BROTHER AND SISTER

My sister always annoys me,
She is such a pain,
My brother hardly annoys me,
But I feel like throwing my sister down a drain.

She never does as she's been told,
And says 'I wish I was in my teens,
So I could be the boss,
And so I could act like the lovely queen.'

When my brother does his homework,
And gets a mistake,
She goes up to him,
And says 'I want to throw you in a lake.'

The only time she is kind,
Is when she wants something from me,
Every night she goes to her room,
And that's when I have a nice cup of tea.

When I'm doing my homework,
She comes and sits beside me,
She says things like,
'That's easy I should be at the academy.'
She thinks she's the best,
But I know she's nothing but a pest.

Alia Ali (13)
Bo'ness Academy

STARS

I looked at the sky one night
one little star looked down
on me!

Then one by one more appeared
all looking at me!

I shut my eyes and looked again
more stars were looking at me!

I thought how many are there
hundreds, thousands?
All looking
at me!

Amy Sorley (12)
Bo'ness Academy

EVACUEE

E vacuation is so sad
V ery unhappy I leave my home and country land
A sleep I lie like a teddy bear
C hug chug but then we stopped
U nhappy we got off the train
E ventually we were taken in
E vacuation is so sad.

Charles Green (13)
Bo'ness Academy

LOST IN SPACE

Like a small child lost
in a dark black night

Floating like a feather
hopelessly in the dark sky

Like a drifting piece of
foil in the dead sea

A little tin box struggling
against the currents
of the fierce rapids.

A little crumb with all
the weight of the galaxy
on its crumbling back

Like a little ant lost
in darkness

A little balloon floating
away from the lost child.

Alastair Tully (12)
Bo'ness Academy

HAIKU: THE GOLDFISH

Swims around all day,
At the bottom of the tank,
The peaceful goldfish.

Kyle Bellamy (12)
Boroughmuir High School

PASTIME

To me life seems a peculiar thing
For though it's incredibly long,
The days just seem to fly right by
But wait, have I got something wrong?

For if a day is but very short,
Then the months must be quite quick
Years and decades go smoothly past
But is life really so slick?

Before I know it I may be dead -
Saving accident or worse -
When my life would be but a blur
And my death a dreadful curse . . .

To those that I will leave behind
To pay for the funeral of course!
But will my murderer have the time
To come and show remorse?

For to us, these days, time is precious
Especially to those in school,
Where lessons most certainly are tedious,
But when late I feel a fool.

So to waste time in the modern world
Is for which we swim or sink,
Bet you feel you've wasted time

- about a minute I think.

Alasdair Raffe (16)
Boroughmuir High School

WINTER

W inds so strong they blow you over
I cicles which hang above your windowpane with a sparkle
N early Christmas and seeing relatives
T oday's the day when the wind is strong and the snow is white
E vergreens will soon fade into a cloud of white
R elatives come over to celebrate the new year.

Laura Turner (12)
Boroughmuir High School

THE RAINFOREST

Please save the rainforest trees,
People there need them more
than we do, so please,
Mahogany doors,
And new parquet floors,
Are not as important as these.

Kerry Dudgeon (12)
Boroughmuir High School

WAR

W ar is a time of hurting.
A rmies constantly fighting day and night.
R aging guns and tanks.

Johnathan Cockroft (12)
Boroughmuir High School

FRIENDSHIP

F orever together
R inging them on the phone
I n their company
E verlasting happiness
N ever apart
D eath doesn't separate
S haring secrets
H aving a great time
I n clubs
P laying games together.

Maxine Cormack (12)
Boroughmuir High School

FEAR

It is I who rides through the dark night,
On my jet-black steed,
I can strike terror into every living thing,
For it is monsters of destruction that I lead,
I stand tall with jet-black hair,
With my black flowing cape,
Every cry I hear,
Be afraid, very afraid.

William Crichton (11)
Boroughmuir High School

SADNESS

Cold and sad are you
Why are you upset
Why are you sad and
blue
Are you lost and
alone
The sun is shining
all around
But it's raining
above you
Tears are trickling
Making puddles on
the floor
Splish splosh!

Sarah Edmonds (12)
Boroughmuir High School

FEAR

When someone is alone at night,
I'll be there like a flash of the light.
As I open the door with the stolen key,
I shout 'Ha ha! You're coming with me!'
I am tall, skinny and have no mates,
Because I'm the leader everyone hates.
I'm fear!

Elaine Scott (12)
Boroughmuir High School

HAUNTED HOUSE

The grandfather clock chimes at midnight,
Signalling the approach of the witching hour.
Ghouls, witches and warlocks come out of the silvery moon
Shadows dance to the cursing tune.
The black souls leave their resting place
And whiz around in open space.
They wander through in and out of rooms,
Wreaking havoc to bring about doom.

When suddenly, as dawn breaks
Spirits freak!
Every dreaded thing hides from the blazing light,
Screaming and roaring with fright.
They're sucked back into their graves
As they all give goodbye waves.

Nafisah Tariq (13)
Boroughmuir High School

DO *NOT* DISTURB!

Suzi's bedroom,
Do not disturb,
She'll be sleeping,
And does not want to be heard,
When she wakes,
She has a big stretch,
But when you throw the bone,
She'll not go and fetch.

Andrew Brown (12)
Boroughmuir High School

HAMSTER

Looking out through the bars of my cage.
Doomed to live my life in this horrid, horrid maze.
As I gaze at the freedom you have,
I wonder how you'd feel.
Trapped like a rat in a trap,
As I run on my little wheel.
Day
Night
Night
Day
Always the same . . . same . . . same.

Christopher Main (13)
Boroughmuir High School

LIFE

Life is just a part of us,
We know we live
But we do not know why.
We are special in our own way,
Some have a kind way,
Some just like their pay.
We live but do not respect life itself
Because life itself does not respect us.

Niall Robert Mackay (12)
Boroughmuir High School

RAIN

Rain rain pouring down
Causing people to wear a frown
All those sellers right down town
Having to close down

But rain can be a real good thing
Helping seeds to grow in spring
Providing water to peasant and king
Making Aboriginal rain dancers sing

Torrential rain will cause a flood
Freezing rain will chill the blood
Turning pastures into mud
But still helping to flower the bud

Beating on the windowpane
The drips are driving me insane
Hoping it will stop in vain
Oh why won't the sun come out again

Rain. Sometimes it makes me quite frustrated
But its majesty is not to be understated
Hail the powers on high ordain
Long may it reign.

Craig Sharp (13)
Boroughmuir High School

SPORTS!

People play all kinds of sports
Games on fields, tracks and courts
People play games with balls
They run, tackle and shoot into goals
People play sports and get lots of fame
They all say it isn't just a game
People play sports and cheat to win
But then it's no fun and they drop the game in the bin
People play sports to have fun
It would be boring to play none.

Robbie Porter (13)
Boroughmuir High School

CHRISTMAS TIME

Outside the snow is falling
Inside the children sleep
Outside the robins are calling
Inside the reindeer peep
Outside Santa Claus will fly
Inside the fire is on
Outside the dog will lie
Inside the cat will yawn.

Genevieve Ryan (13)
Boroughmuir High School

PRESSURE

You're under and you can't get out,
It's not just something you can just miss out,
It is not what you want to be,
It is what you are but not to be,

We can see you,
But we can't help out,
It is your life,
And you are living it on the edge of a knife,

You are staring straight at a brick wall,
You have nothing,
When you could have had it all,

After we've all gone away,
You'll be there;
Withering in the pain,

You've got to help yourself today,
Otherwise you will have to pay.

Ross Robertson (13)
Boroughmuir High School

PEACE

P eople together in harmony.
E veryone meditating together.
A nyone can join in it's perfectly free.
C almness all around.
E veryone in harmony.

Kirsty Theobald (12)
Boroughmuir High School

DETACHMENT

Detachment smothers me
Like a brick wall
With me on one side and normals on the other
My detachment cell has two windows
So I can see what I'm missing
What others take for granted
Is forbidden to me

Those who do speak to me
See me as a pitiable soul
Frustration boils up inside me
I want to scream, I want to shout
But have no way to let it out
I want people to understand
That inside this useless body
I still have a brain and a mind.

Alison Shepherd (12)
Boroughmuir High School

DESERT

Deserted landscape
Still and calm
Nothing but sand and stones
Thirst-quenching heat
Hot and tired
No movement
Just still and calm.

Amanda McNeil (12)
Boroughmuir High School

THE JUNGLE

To me, day and night are the same:
Forever darkness.
I am alive with movement
But the sound of the outside world I miss.
Oh how I wish.

Then suddenly I hear a noise,
An awful, terrible sound.
I have to get out,
Or for help I should shout -
Something is eating the ground,
But my mouth stays permanently shut.

As I begin to fall
Inside my head I scream.
But no one will listen,
Nobody cares.
So I silently call,
And the pain begins.

Now I am quiet,
I have nothing to say.
I have a stick with a ball that does sway,
A slow, even noise is emanating from inside me.
Tick-tock, tick-tock . . .

Tariq Ashkanani (12)
Boroughmuir High School

HELLO?

Is anyone there?
I'm alone,
With nothing but air.
No mother to defend me,
No one to befriend me.

I'm alone.
Does anyone care?

Hello?
Is anyone there?

Xian Li (11)
Boroughmuir High School

WIND

With blows,
And gales,
It fills the sails.

It bends the trees,
And makes them sway,
With great big swirls,
It curls the sea,
That makes the waves,
To sail away,
From March to May,
Until today.

Louise Cumming (13)
Boroughmuir High School

TEARDROP

Salty tears that fall like rain,
Tears of hurt,
Tears of pain.
Drops of water that do twinkle,
From the eye they make a sprinkle.
They fall down in marvellous twirls,
Some in twists,
Some in swirls,
Through your eyes they will seep,
So close your eyes and do not weep!
When they roll down your cheek,
They look like a winding,
Entwining creek.
As the teardrop splashes to the ground,
A little crystal there shall be found.

Ellie Jones (13)
Boroughmuir High School

SCHOOL

S chool is so incredibly boring
C afeteria meals are yuck!
H ow I put up with it I don't know . . .
O h I nearly fell asleep in English
O h I nearly snored in history.
L ast thing it is time to go and it really makes my day.

James Allen (12)
Boroughmuir High School

MY DREAM

My box holds a dream
A dream only I can dream
It swirls and whirls around
And only I can see it

It is made of dust
Magic, sparkling dust
That holds the dream inside
And keeps it safe

Now I will hide my box
Hide it from anyone else
Because it's my dream
And only I'm going to dream it.

Rachael Ellis (11)
Boroughmuir High School

FEELINGS

A glimmer of hope shines through sadness
Happiness breaks through despair
Optimism overcomes denial
You are always there
Cupid helps you through anger
Confidence turns away threat
Mystery controls danger
Nothing contradicts that.

Sarah Wann (13)
Boroughmuir High School

WAR

People killed and wounded,
Children all alone with no parents,
I don't think that war is right,
Do you?
Why do we kill people that we don't even know,
For no reason except the fact that we're told to?
I don't think that war is right,
Do you?
What would the world be like if there were no more wars?
I'll bet that it would be a happier, safer place.
I don't think that war is right,
Do you?

Jennifer Paton (13)
Boroughmuir High School

WHOSE BOX IS IT?

I have a box, but I don't own it,
I live in it, but it is not mine.
It is big outside, and small inside
Whose box is it?

The box isn't mine, it belongs to the Jones'.
They threw it out a few weeks ago.
It used to house a brand-new freezer,
But now it is in the kitchen.
The box was mine for the taking,
I saw my chance and I seized it.

Andrew Murdoch (12)
Boroughmuir High School

LEAVES

First I am green
To change I am keen
In autumn I'm red
Before I am dead
Softly I fall to the ground
Stand on me I make a crunching sound.

Tom McCallum (12)
Boroughmuir High School

SUMMER

Summertime is hot!
Summer is a happy time!
I like summertime!

Jemma Handren (11)
Boroughmuir High School

ROBIN

The robin in the tree
As it looks straight at me
The snow falls, it flies away.

Nicole Bourke (11)
Boroughmuir High School

FALLING LEAVES

Why do the leaves fall glumly from the trees?
And the raindrops lash out in bitter remorse
Why does summer's warm beckoning and hot passion freeze?
Yet still hold me in its grasp, but, of course,
Even life's secure hopes seem destined to fail.
Love turns to hate, happiness to fear.
Winter envelopes its menace behind a sparkling veil.
No one sees the puddles freeze and wind howl this year,
The cold bite like a bullet and the brashness of the rain.
They dance around, all merry, while I glance back on summer,
They don't perceive the darkness or feel the monotonous pain,
Don't notice the grey clouds getting greyer and glummer.

Esther Sced (15)
Boroughmuir High School

BOX

My box
Made of laughter
Inside there is a friend, an alien friend
As I touch the box I have fun
I hear a whoosh
And I go in and see a green figure
With beady golden eyes
And eight bony fingers
I keep it as a secret so that I can have it all to myself
I have excitement when I'm there
It's like a different atmosphere
Fun, exciting, crazy and almost irresistible.

Katrina Cowie (12)
Boroughmuir High School

THE BOX

My box is made of imagination
It changes every time you look
Whenever the box is opened
The imaginative thoughts appear
They dive into your head
Making you dream
Of lovely things like sweets and ice-cream
But if you have no imagination
You're stuck-up and self-centred
And you open the box
Then you're entering doom
Because there are no sweets
Just a deadly and dark gloom
From every corner of the earth
Come ghosts, ghouls and corpses!
You're surrounded
And they want to kill
They are chanting a chant
That gives you the chills
Help! Help! Help! You cry
For you only have minutes
Till you'll surely die.

Daniel Gibb (12)
Boroughmuir High School

MY SHOES

My box is very small
it holds my first pair of shoes
it's so small I keep it in my pencil case
and take it to school every day.

My box is made of a blue ribbon
which ties the two shoes together
so I don't lose one because they
are so special.

I am the only one who knows
about this box because I want
it to be my little secret.

Charlotte Nicholl (11)
Boroughmuir High School

THE BULL

As warm as the sun,
As cold as ice,
As hard as rock,
As big as Mount Everest,
As small as a flea,
As old as a tomb,
As young as a midget,
As stupid as a baby,
As smart as a wizard.

Keith Roberts (11)
Boroughmuir High School

UNTITLED

Red is for love
Yellow is for the sun in the sky
Green is for the grass that lies upon the ground
Purple is my favourite colour of all
Blue is for a bright summer's day
Pink is the colour of my flesh
Brown is for the chocolate I eat
Black is boring and dull
Peach is as juicy as me and you
Lilac is for beauty
White is as white as the paper I write upon
Grey is as dull as the sky at night
Silver is as sleek as the moon at sleep
Maroon is the team me and you love.

Katie Goodwin & Irene Massaquoi (13)
Boroughmuir High School

THE SPIRIT

There's something inside me,
that's pounding to get out.
A spirit that's been left with
a lonely doubt.
A hole in someone's life
a space that can't be filled.
There's a spirit inside me
One day it might get out.

Katie M Dawson (13)
Boroughmuir High School

THE TEACHERS OF B'MUIR

In the school B'Muir
The teachers are pure
Some are pure nasty
Some are pure cool
And some just drool.

Some teach us French
And the ones that do gym make us sit on a bench
Some let you eat
And some let you speak.

Others just moan
And others groan
Teachers in English make us write
All day and if they had their way
All night as well.

You go into the staff room
And you never hear music booming
They have a big comfy seat
Where they sit and have something to eat.

Sandy McCaskey (14)
Boroughmuir High School

LIGHT AND DARK

Dark at night can give you a fright,
Light in the night, oh what a sight,
Dark and light are always in a conflict,
But light always wins this fight.

Pedrum Aval (12)
Boroughmuir High School

NEW YORK

New York, New York
or otherwise the Big Apple
huge, scary
lots of traffic, noise and yellow cabs
busy people rushing by
they would not even tell me
where Bloomingdale's or Sears is,
they just look then carry on walking.
How I wish I was back at home!
People sleeping on the street in boxes,
on the rubbish
rats scurrying beside the homeless,
how I would hate to live like that.

Joanna Redpath (14)
Boroughmuir High School

HOW WOULD YOU FEEL?

How would you feel if you:
Worked all day,
Without any pay,
Sometimes with no food,
Employers in an awful mood,
If they want to kick,
It's you they pick,
I want to be free,
To swim in the sea,
Or soar like an eagle,
This cannot be legal.

Anne Somerville (13)
Boroughmuir High School

THE DRAGON

Its fiery breath that brings the death
upon a mortal soul
knight with lance tries to advance
and his body is turned to coal.

In his underground cave lies the body of a slave
death and destruction all about
he lies and dreams remembering the screams
smoke coming out of his snout.

He likes to kill it gives him a thrill
he went hunting in the month of May
people lay dead the stream ran red
on that horrible, bloody day.

Flying high picking birds out the sky
a meal that does not last
people try to run he flies under the sun
the deadly shadow is cast.

He has a desire to start a fire
and watch the people burn
he lights a fag and an old hag
and sees her toss and turn.

Some hunters come each holding a gun
and shoot the beast from the sky
he circles round falling to the ground
and they watch him slowly die.

The villagers rejoice but hear an evil voice
two shadows are cast below
his mummy and daddy are very unhappy
and have come to kill their foe.

Matthew Clark & Patrick Simpson (13)
Boroughmuir High School

WISHFUL THINKING

Everything was silent in the school,
Except for the scrape of a Science stool.
Then Lucy cried, 'My experiment's gone wrong!
My beaker's letting off a terrible pong!'

'Uh, oh,' said the teacher, quaking in fear,
'The liquid should be brown and certainly not clear!
It shouldn't be steaming and fizzing like so,
If you ask my opinion - I think it'll blow!'

The beaker then cracked and the liquid poured out,
'Oh cool! No more school!' little Lucy did shout.
The liquid turned purple then orange, then blue,
The scared teacher shouted, 'Oh what shall we do?'

The school soon violently burst into flames,
As usual the pupils got most of the blame.
The teacher informed them, as he felt they must know,
'Sadly there's no school for a few months or so!'

Lindsay Sharp (13)
Boroughmuir High School

HOMEWORK

Why do I have to do work at home?
That is why they created school
You are totally defeating the point
If you obey the homework rule

I work six hours a day
I am happy to get home
I can spend hours watching TV
Or around the streets I can roam

Yeah right, in my dreams
I have to do work every night
This whole thing is getting out of hand
It really isn't right.

Patrick Simpson (13)
Boroughmuir High School

SNEAKY PEEK

Twinkly lights on the Christmas tree
Bushy, sparkly and tinselly
A pile of presents growing
Outside the snow is blowing

I pick up a little red box
And quickly look up at the clock
Feeling guilty and meek
No one is in to see me peek

I give it a shake
I hope it won't break
I give it a spin
Is there anything within?

I really don't know what's inside
'Uh oh,' I've been spied
'What are you doing you silly girl?
Leave the pressies alone
Or you'll get none!'

'Whoops.'

Rona Crawley (13)
Boroughmuir High School

THE CLASSROOM

Sitting in the classroom,
Staring all around,
Looking out the window
Seeing snow fluttering down
Desperate to get out there
But still so long to go
Sitting here,
Whilst the teacher keeps on talking,
I sit feeling glum,
Wishing I was outside
Playing in the snow.
Suddenly I hear the teacher say,
'Right, it's time to go!'

Rachel Craik (13)
Boroughmuir High School

HOMELESS

My box is cold and I have nothing to eat,
I've been battered and I have had no sleep.
I see rich people walking on the beat
While I sit and watch the world go by.
I hate this world, there's no place to go,
It makes me feel really low.
I sleep in the gutter,
I sleep in the street,
I feel sick and I've got freezing cold feet.

Matthew Stevenson (13)
Boroughmuir High School

GRANDMA

I see her lying on the bed
And pray to God that she is not dead
But I know she can not be
I can see her heart beating in front of me.

I sit beside her and hold her hand
As she tells me of her dream in the sand
The tears start running down her face
She tells me of this wonderful place.

The monitor starts bleeping
I thought she was just sleeping
As I remember the words in my head
I know that she is really dead.

Rachael Docking (12) & Lizzy Hill (13)
Boroughmuir High School

ALONE

My eyes start filling up with water
All my friends start laughing
I feel left out and embarrassed
I run away to a place where I belong
The streets.

I am homeless, scared and unwanted
I have no food or money
People don't care about me
I am a nobody
I am alone.

Natalie Phillips (13)
Boroughmuir High School

CHRISTMAS THOUGHTS

It's dark,
Cold and damp,
It rains and rains,
Colder now.
Snow is coming
Christmas is nearer.
I like the snow
Christmas is fun
Warm and friendly
Although I can't wait until
The sun shines again,
When it's warm,
Say 'Goodbye' to the snow.

Holly Thornthwaite (13)
Boroughmuir High School

CHRISTMAS

I stand beside my Christmas tree
Staring at it joyfully
With the twinkling lights
So peaceful, so bright
The angel sitting at the top
As if she is the queen of pop
All the presents and decoration
What a terrific celebration.

Laura Sutherland (13)
Boroughmuir High School

There Must Be Something . . .

What to write?
I can't think
My mind's gone blank
'Write a poem,' the teacher said
'What about?' I thought, in my head
All my class mates
Have great ideas
Diana, memories, and Christmas cheer
But I am just left sitting here.
Sitting here I feel so bored
I think I'm going to fall asleep
But I need to think of something quick
'Only fifteen minutes left,'
The teacher calls from behind his desk
There must be something I can write
Poetry, 'Oh I give up!'
I absolutely hate the stuff!

Anne Strachan (13)
Boroughmuir High School

Homeless

I'm sitting there, no one to care
No money to spend it isn't fair
People walk past day and night
And they stare at you and think what a sight
Some nights I sit and moan
But most of all I'm all alone.

Craig Carr (13)
Boroughmuir High School

WINTER IN EDINBURGH

Cold, damp, dark nights,
Wandering down the moonlit streets,
Severe, glaring orange lights staring down at us,

Cold, crisp winter mornings,
Wrap up warm with hats, gloves and scarves,
Snow fluttering from a clear blue sky,

Colds, flu and winter bugs,
Warm drinks in front of the fire,
Soon you feel better,

Christmas comes,
Walking round the shops,
Santa Claus brings presents,

Christmas has come,
Wrapping paper everywhere,
Snow covering the ground, like a white blanket.

Elizabeth Dunn (13)
Boroughmuir High School

MY FRIEND

The loss of her life touched the bottom of my heart,
My feelings for her will never depart,
As I walk through the cold night air,
I think of her as if she was there,
But she's not,
She's gone.

She would never, ever be mean,
The greatest wonder life has ever seen.
Helping people through night and day,
I wish she never went away,
But she did,
She's gone.

Louise Bingham (13)
Boroughmuir High School

FEELING ILL

'She is ill' I hear the doctor say
May not last another day.
Outside everyone is having fun
I'll be the only one to die so young.
I'm scared to go away to sleep
In case I never wake up again.
Then I think, maybe it would be for the best
To give my poor Mother a rest
From all the hassle, all the grief
I think I'll go and have a sleep
And see where I end up in the morning
Will I be here alive
Or away somewhere else
Dead . . .

Sasha Watson (12)
Boroughmuir High School

THE DESK

The desk is a magical desk,
With a magical scratch on the top.
The desk is made out of magical wood,
And magical metal.

People have vandalised the magical desk,
With graffiti and chewing gum.
People must feel that the desk has no feelings,
That it does not wish to look good.

Each day I sit at this magical desk,
Slaving away at my work,
I look at the magical scratch and graffiti,
And wish they could disappear.

Iain Welsh (13)
Boroughmuir High School

FRIZZLING FIREWORKS

Frizzling fireworks fizzing for far,
Silver sparklers shining around,
Magnificent moon mimicking the sun,
Petrified pets hiding under the bed!

Christmas crackers cracking all day,
Tremendous turkey, I can't wait,
Perfect presents being played till they break,
Long letter thanking all those aunts and uncles!

Ian Somerville (12)
Boroughmuir High School

QUESTION?

Who are you?
I am something.
What's your name?
My name is nothing.
Where do you live?
I live somewhere of nowhere.
How old are you?
I am ageless.
How tall are you?
I am taller than the sky.
What weight are you?
I am lighter than dust.

Bruce Kung (13)
Boroughmuir High School

MATHS TEST

Ticking brains
Rulers
Scraping pencils
People measuring in millimetres
Nerves
Writing names back to front
Pencil sharpeners
Rubbers
Vibrating pens
Wobbling knees, shaking desks
That was a horrible maths test!

Sarah Craig (13)
Broxburn Academy

MY BROTHER

We call him wee Ally
He is my little bro
Just what we did without him
I really do not know

He just had his first birthday
Now he's trying to walk
He's pretty good at shouting
But I am teaching him to talk

He loves to ha a swalley
And sit upon my knee
I tell him Ally Bally
He smiles up at me

He has to wear a nappy
To use it for the loo
This seems to make him happy
I wish he could change it too.

Jake Duncan (13)
Broxburn Academy

THE FREE KICK

I stepped back
I picked my place
I gave it a good smack
The ball went through the space

Faster than the speed of sound
Like a shooting star
It was surely goal-bound
But it hit the bar

The keeper couldn't believe it
Neither could I
I felt like Jorg Albertz a bit
But I still want to cry.

Gary Callaghan (12)
Broxburn Academy

THE SPARROW AND THE DRAGONFLY

'Twas a sparrow in a tree
Looking for its tea
When then in the sky
It saw a dragonfly

After the insect the hungry bird flew
How long the chase would last, neither had a clue
The sparrow swooped and dived after its prey
And hopes of the fly surviving began to fade away

As the chase went on, the bug began to tire
Until it heard a certain noise and began to fly higher
Up and up, into a cloud
And when they came out of it the noise was really loud

The culprit of the noise was a very large plane
And the dragonfly headed for its propeller, as if it were insane
On its deadly flight it stayed
Until the very last second, when to the left it strayed

Alas the sparrow flew straight on
Into the propeller and he was gone.

Rory Anderson (13)
Broxburn Academy

BEING LATE

I woke up late for school
I didn't want to go
I begged my mum 'Please'
But she said 'No'

I jumped out of bed
And brushed my hair
Put on some clothes
And dived downstairs

As I arrived at school
I found that no one was there
I looked in the classroom
It was bare!

I turned back in despair
And realised I shouldn't be here
And in fact the school was closed
For the summer fare!

Claire Widdowson (13)
Broxburn Academy

OLD AGE

Oh, how I'd hate to be old
teeth all ugly and battered
life begins at sixty so I'm told
but that's just a load of patter

Christmas at old age
gloves, hankies and socks
personally what I'd really like
is to be buried in a box

Going up the road in your buggy
to collect your pension
get it out your local post office,
mind, that I forgot to mention.

Nicky Reid (13)
Broxburn Academy

TRUE NIGHTMARE

Pressure when I came in the school gates,
Seeing her standing there waiting,
There's no way out, I try to hide,
I can't help it, but I am shaking.

She walks to me with a growl,
She steals my school dinner money,
She teases me about how I wear a brace,
And thinks all this is very funny.

I run as fast as I can,
Not turning round to see her,
I manage to stop, panting for breath,
I turn around and she's still there.

I get pushed to the ground,
Get up, get up, get up.
I open my eyes,
I've just woke up.

It was all a bad dream,
The memory comes back
The bully will be waiting
To renew her attack.

Cleo Pace (13)
Broxburn Academy

THE SEAGULLS

Flying, soaring very high,
Droppings coming from the sky,
Hitting people by the dozen,
Even splattered my big cousin.

Scattered people looking white,
Because of droppings not of fright,
Seagulls swooping down and down,
Annoying people in the town.

Stealing bread and stealing chips,
Even stealing sherbet dips,
One seagull grabbed my buttered roll,
Then flew off and ate it whole.

When eating goodies on the beach,
Keep them out of seagulls' reach,
But don't use violence and don't use a gun,
On public enemy number one!

Scott Harris (12)
Broxburn Academy

MY MUM

My mum's name is Helen
She looks quite like Cher
She is very tall
With long, dark hair.

My mum has some bad habits
She smokes like a chimney
But when I tell her to stop
She looks at me grimly.

She takes me out places
That I like to go
She buys me lots of presents
Because she loves me so.

My mum can be moany
But I don't care
Because when I need help
My mum's always there.

Stephanie Perry (12)
Broxburn Academy

ALIENS

The aliens are coming,
we all better run and hide.

Here their spaceship comes
but they don't have their engines on.
You can see them glide over our planet.

The aliens are landing,
the military draw their tails.

The spaceship lands,
we all gaze at a sign, it says USA.

A man gets out and says
'We come in peace for all mankind
from the planet Earth.'

Callum Turnbull (12)
Broxburn Academy

MY SISTER

My sister's really moody
She never seems to smile,
When I mention tidying up
She moans, then runs a mile.

She never, ever listens
To what I have to say,
I ask her simple questions
But she just screams 'Go away!'

Although she has her bad points
I simply can't complain,
When she gives me money
And helps when I'm in pain.

She can be very helpful
When I'm stuck on maths,
We have good times together
And many, many laughs.

So after all, I suppose
She isn't all that bad,
She's the best big sister
That I have ever had.

Holly Matthews (12)
Broxburn Academy

FOODS

Mince and tatties, custard and mustard,
Cannelloni,
Ravioli,
Boiled eggs,
And chicken legs,
Fish and chips,
Weetabix,
A jam piece,
A round of quiche,
Haddock in batter,
Wi a drap ae watter,
Some mushy peas,
Mozzarella cheese,
For breakfast Cornflakes,
And cheese cakes,
Bourbon creams,
Jelly beans,
Toffee and coffee,
Mince pies, frogs' eyes,
Fizzy lemonade,
And marmalade,
Yum, yum, yum.

David Smith (13)
Broxburn Academy

My Dog

My dog's name is Chico,
It's quite a silly name,
And whenever something happens
He always gets the blame.

Chico's small and hairy,
He's like a teddy bear,
He chases all the cats,
And he really doesn't care.

He runs about the house,
With a squeaky toy,
He squeaks it all day long,
And it really does annoy.

Chico barks loudly,
When he hears a noise outside.
He'll wake you up if you're asleep,
And then he'll go and hide.

Tracey Craik (12)
Broxburn Academy

Clouds

What is a cloud -
doesn't everybody wonder?
I think it is a pillow for angels to lie upon,
or maybe it is a ball of candyfloss,
hanging from an invisible stick.
What is a cloud?
Is it a cradle for a baby to sleep in;
or a store room for happiness to lie?

What is a cloud?
Is it balls of cotton wool floating in the sky,
and falling as snow?
What is a cloud?
Is it an angel's knitting slowly being
put into the cupboard,
so the sun can come out?

Jemma Finlayson (12)
Deans Community High School

TEARDROP

She lay in her room
upset and alone.
Her stomach felt like a box of butterflies
that had been let loose.

A tear fell from her eye
it was like silver
shining in the moonlight.
It sparkled and gave out rays of light
around the room.

She slowly lifted up her finger
and caught the tear.
She had it lying on her finger like a small insect
with no movement - no life -
just a clear motionless figure
that slowly disappeared and left no sparkle
left no shine.

Laura Ramage (15)
Deans Community High School

COLOURS

When I'm relaxing,
blue, green and turquoise
laze around in my head.

When I'm happy,
yellow, pink and peach
play around in my head.

When I'm upset,
black, grey and white
flow around in my head.

When I'm furious,
red, orange and maroon
race in my head.

Craig Stewart (13)
Deans Community High School

SILVER

Shining silver in the night,
from the glistening moon.
Shining upon the lake,
So calm,
So still,
My nails shine under the great moon.
But slowly,
Very slowly,
It fades.
My tears drop upon the damp ground
as the dawn awakes.

Lesley Ann Allan (13)
Deans Community High School

WATER

From conception to extinction - water is life.
Without the luxury of water we would all be in strife.
I don't really remember, but I am told,
Me playing in the bath was a sight to behold!
I would kick and splash and giggle with glee
Being surrounded by water set me free.
I remember jumping in puddles and playing in the rain,
Getting covered in muck, well I'm not vain!
Going to the beach was always a delight,
Chasing the waves oh what a sight.
Exploring rock pools for crabs, seaweed and shells
Is a holiday pastime I remember so well.
Water fights on hot summer days
Cooled us down from the ultraviolet rays.
Water slide, flumes and swimming in the sea
Are fun ways to pass the time for you and for me.
But always remember, never forget,
The danger that lurks beneath its depths.
As the tide ebbs and flows, and the waterfall roars,
A secret is skulking where no one knows.
Torrential rain creates floods,
Drought creates famine and disease.
Man should respect water and not regard it with ease;
We should treasure this life source - not do as we please.

Martin Stirling (15)
Deans Community High School

THE BOX

Shattered, my mind is blown.
Every memento of my dream I'm packing up.
I put my heart and reputation on the line
And now I'm drowning in my tears.

Photos, gifts and happiness -
They are all packed up.
Tears have happiness washed away.
Now they are in a cardboard box.

In the light of a full moon
My box is burned to a cinder.
At twelve midnight the flames calm down
And the wind scatters the ashes.

Robert Packwood (14)
Deans Community High School

WHAT IS . . . THE MOON

The moon is a silvery ball,
which lies there in the dark.
It shines like a light and is
cold in the morning, warm in the evening.

It is a shiny coin that someone has
dropped from heaven.
It is like a pumpkin waiting
patiently for Hallowe'en to come.

The moon comes up every night
staying in that same spot
up in the sky.
Waiting patiently to die.

Kirsty Hamill (12)
Deans Community High School

THE JOURNEY ALONG THE TRODDEN LEAVES

Oh whatever shall I do?
My little paws are turning blue!
My homely hole in the ground,
A tiny little cosy mound,
Is completely covered in winter snow.

Burrow, burrow, dig, dig,
I excavate the sunken twigs,
It's so cold and I need fuel,
But please don't think I am a fool,
For I did not know it would snow.

I have a little food reserved,
But how long will it stay preserved?
I'm scared I'll be trapped in my tiny home,
Underneath this snowy dome,
For many weeks to come.

Alas! I have made a hole!
Now I can search for coal!
Food! Food! Come to me!
With this haze it's hard to see,
But I still have my tingling nose.

Paddling through decaying leaves and twigs,
I stop and nibble at the figs.
Sliding along the icy puddles,
Sometimes I get in awful muddles!
Now I shall return home.

I am thankful I returned safely,
Oh, I do wish there was a hedgehog Safeway!
I shall now roll into a snug-tight ball,
And pretend winter didn't come at all.

Valerie Gibson (13)
Deans Community High School

WATER BABIES

On a wave of coldness,
This silence of years,
But you can never complain
About your path of tears.
Break onto this wavelength,
Fall off your fears,
Destroy all comfort,
And regret your tears.
Swim free my friend.

But the Water Babies
They'll never know,
And never wonder,
Because they never grow.

Swung deep from the unborn,
Blind drunk on dreams,
And this dearth of despair
Bursts at the seams.
And though it is clueless
It knows you well,
Fills you with darkness,
From heaven, from hell.
Swim on my friend.

But the Water Babies
They'll never know,
And never wonder,
Because they never grow.

He'll never leave;
Hunger owns his soul,
Because the Water Babies
Just take him low.
Swim deep my friend.

Nicol Hay (17)
Deans Community High School

THE GIFT

My gift would be a remedy,
To last a whole life long.
It would give you the freedom
You'd always dreamed of,
And keep you healthy and strong.

My gift would cure your illness,
Make all your dreams come true.
You deserve it -
The most remarkable person
On earth has got to be you.

My gift would stop the injections,
The sugar count each day.
It would banish all your
Fears of blindness
And ill health far away.

It's yours because I love you,
Always have and always will.
It's yours because you are
A tower of strength,
Even though you are ill.

Laura McConnell (15)
Deans Community High School

EGG

An oval, moulded by a tight shell,
a speckled sphere,

cracked,

into a sizzling bath of hot oil,
revealing a golden coin shining through a snowy cloud.

Then flipped onto a rough slab,
the lava oozes out,
distorting the purity of the cloud.

A soldier plunges in,
spreading the lava in all directions,
like a sunshine river flowing calmly towards the sea.

It enters the deep pothole.
All is dark.
The rough surface of the red road pushes upwards,
      falling,
            falling,
in through the grey pipe,
into a vast, cold, dark cave.

Eilidh Hall (12)
Fettes College

BOARDING

Unrelenting pain in your stomach,
Growing larger as the days go on.
Having a daily routine,
And knowing you'll never return.

Then, going back to España again,
Seeing your family at the half-term.
It's no big shakes, no big deal,
In fact you find that you want to return.

Rebecca Hitchen (11)
Fettes College

TRAVELLING NIGHT

Night moves on,
Through cities.
Street lamps glow,
Shadows drape,
Lending themselves to the light.

As it swoops and glides,
Night catches its prey.
The land is captured,
Then left lying,
Silent and numb.

It descends on the ocean.
Midnight falls heavily,
But makes no sound.
Gentle waves purl,
Glinting in the mottled moonlight.

The cool of night drifts away.
Dawn has come.
Earth turns to the sun,
A palette of colours,
Reflecting life.

Hannah Clarke (13)
Fettes College

GONE TO THE CHIP SHOP

Got hardly any money
And I need some food.
Sunday night and the streets are lifeless as a desert.

Everywhere is closed,
Except the local chip shop.

I make my way towards it,
Ravenous as a starving whale,
I keep on walking,
When will I get there?

I turn around the corner,
Hooray!
I see my local chip shop.
I'm walking fast as lightning.

Finally I stumble in,
Immediately feeling the equator-like heat.
Soon I hear the sizzling,
Now I'm thirsty as a dried-up sponge.

I ask for a fish supper,
And within an instant,
The fish was cooked and hot as metal.
She pours the salt on like a snowy blizzard,
Then wraps the fish with ancient newspaper.

I leave the sauna-hot chip shop,
Into the arctic-like night.
I start hiking back,
Towards my shoebox-sized flat.

I begin to eat the vinegar-drenched chips,
Oh, that tastes good.
The rain start to pour like Niagara Falls,
So I quicken up my pace.

Eventually I reach my block,
I enter my flat,
Turn on the TV
And eat my delicious fish supper.

Melvin Byres (13)
Fettes College

THE SEA

Quiet and calm, all blues and greens,
Like a soft baby's blanket half-covering the world.
Lapping gently against the rocks,
Like a cat licking up milk.
All is peaceful and still.

But suddenly death-black clouds appear
Marching forward like a fierce army before a battle.
The old, violent wind gets up and blows a riot.
The waves swell up and turn jet-black.
With fierce cut-throat white daggers,
Coming crashing onto the beach,
Like galloping horses commencing a race,
Or a pack of hungry wolves pouncing on their prey.

Then slowly the calm begins to settle,
Like a hoary fog descending on a dark, foreign land.
The wind recoils into its cold, dusky layer.

Camilla McCorkell (12)
Fettes College

A Deathly Silence

The words close in on me,
trapping me.
She is dead,
gone from my sight.
It locks and furls around me.
No, she has just moved on,
gone into the next room.
The door is closed now.
Silence,
the whole world is silent,
everything is dead.
She can't come back,
she is a vessel,
gone from my sight.
We are sad as we wave goodbye.
But when she reaches her destination,
happy shouts fill the air.
I must now wait to make the same journey.
Silence,
I break it,
I want to hit and throw everything in sight.
I press my face into my pillow,
making muffled cries of agony.
The never-ending feeling,
of wanting to touch and to hold,
is tearing me apart.
I hear nothing,
everything is gone.
Silence,
A deathly silence.

Emma-Kate Hunter (12)
Fettes College

STORM

The waves are like loads of high peaks,
They frequently change direction,
Never knowing why they should be calm,
They eat the ships like a whale
eating fish.
They have a lot of control,
So they show it to us at the sea.

Wind, the waves' main helper,
Blows like an aeroplane flying,
In the sky at a great speed.
It blows out everything like dynamite exploding
and knocking all out of its way,
without taking any care.

The lightning of course,
Is a useful helper to aid the wind and waves,
It flashes like a photo-flash with a mysterious flicker,
It makes a sound of a battle tank
firing,
with hope to hit his assailant.

So many sailors sank,
Like stones going deeper and deeper
Into the ocean,
Nobody was ever found,
After the ocean had been furious.

Denis Zoubkov (12)
Fettes College

CHRISTMAS EVE

A blanket of snow
covers the ground,
like icing on a cake.
I take a look behind me,
there's a print, each step I take!

Tiny clusters of cotton wool
float gracefully through the air
and plant themselves upon the snow,
entangling themselves in my hair!

Snow-encrusted window sills,
chimneys puffing smoke.
Smiling, happy children,
tumbling upstairs to bed.

Within the icy windowpanes,
are rooms filled with warmth.
Glowing fires lick at the air,
as if thirsty for a drink.

A fairy stands grandly,
on top of the enchanted tree.
Acting as if she is the queen
of all there is to see!

In her magic kingdom,
are lights of every colour.
And silver and gold coloured baubles
reflecting on each other.

Tinsel sparkles brightly
among the twinkly lights,
entwined between the prickly bows.

I glance around behind me
(to make sure I'm out of sight!)
Then squeeze down the chimney pot
(I am as fast as light!)

I fill their little stockings
and put more presents under the tree.
Then I settle down beside the fire
and eat the mince pie left for me!

Fiona Mould (12)
Fettes College

SNORKELLING

The sand-bank of the sea,
So clear, just like glass.
I see the sand-dunes, pint sized but in detail,
While I listen to the sounds
of the inside of a shell.

On I go using my flippers like a whale,
Puff, puff goes the puffer fish
trying to look a fiend,
Flap, flap go the wings of the restive ray
going round in circles.

On, on I go with my blowhole exploding
out aqua into the waves.
To the cliff, like the edge of a canyon,
To see the many complexions of the coral.
The moray eel looking mean, with
a mouth bigger than my mother's.
But now go back, back to leave the secrets
for another day.

Cornelius Dirkzwager (12)
Fettes College

HEADS AND HOOVES

Sunday morning,
Ten o'clock,
They never fail to show.

Sunday morning,
Ten o'clock,
Heads appear round the corner.

Sunday morning,
Ten o'clock,
Galloping hooves tumble by.

Shining leather,
Velvet hats,
Proud riders glide loudly by.

Stretched-out body,
Prancing feet,
Many horses clatter by.

Galloping past,
To the beach,
To show their heads and hooves there.

Tamsin Murley (12)
Fettes College

WINGS

Of all the wondrous things,
I would love to have a pair of wings,
I could fly above the clouds at night,
I could travel across the world in flight,
I would float like a boat on the clouds' endless seas.

Ivor Williams (13)
George Heriot's School

MISS BARKLAY MUIR

She looks on to winter differently.
No fun and games in the snow,
But danger signs,
On icy paths.

What has she got to look forward to?
Another tumble?
'The spring!' She exclaims,
The garden will be bright,
What will it bring for her ninety-first year?

Has it been so long?

She has a lot of time,
To think these days.
Less visits to old friends,
They've all moved on now.
Lots of free time,
Time to think.

She looks optimistically,
To the future ahead,
She's from the old school,
Stiff upper lip and all that.

I can't understand her point of view,
Her optimism,
Seventy-nine years of life separate our thinking.

Neave Corcoran (12)
George Heriot's School

TELEVISION

Telly is a great, great thing,
it helps me to relax.
Although I'm told I watch too much,
I think it really works.

I'm home from school and on it goes,
my favourite little box.
Then in comes Mum and 'zzop' it's gone,
She's switched my telly off.

So off in search of something else,
I go to fulfil my hunger.
But nothing else quite hits the spot,
than Snoopy, from when I was younger.

Sitting in my living room,
eyes are getting square.
What shall I do next, I think,
but then I think who cares?

Simon Donne (14)
George Heriot's School

DOORSTOPS

Two fluffy doorstops
not to be disturbed.
Dreaming of catching fish
or a mouse or a bird.

A cat's only worry is
when it gets its food.
Do not waken a sleeping cat
for that is considered rude.

Their only work is sleeping,
sleeping on the ball.
On a bed or on the floor
or even in the hall.

Peter Black (14)
George Heriot's School

YESTERDAY'S TOWN

The winter dusk
Curtained the village like a thick, heavy cloak.
I felt icy whips of wind tug on my face,
And trickle down my neck.
I stopped.

Memories flooded me with warmth
As I drifted in a dream of years gone by.
Long days spent idly basking in sunshine.
Familiar buzzing and humming of life;
Days now buried deep under folds of time.

The sky looked down hauntingly, down on my
Forgotten town
As if it too were in mourning.
I hesitated.
A final glance told my heart what my head already knew.
I no longer belonged.

Retreating with a heavy heart.
The ghostly wind howling desperately
Pulling and urging me back.
But deep down
My heart had already gone.

Elizabeth Welsh (15)
George Heriot's School

VILLAGE LANDSCAPE IN MORNING LIGHT

Watched over by a troubled, but stable sky.
Guarded by tranquil but substantial forces.
Enveloping life in a passive manner,
And life is good.

Flanked by fertile pastures,
Ideal for gentle pastimes.
At a reasonable distance from civilisation, for freedom,
But within boundaries.

A mighty but imperfect oak gives a brief respite
For a tired and simple man.
His appreciation is limited yet honest and whole.
His flock is patient.

The time for rest will pass eventually,
But exists at the moment, glorious and calm.
All is as it should be, not out of place.
Not perfect but a happy space.

Christian McDermott (15)
George Heriot's School

ERUPTION

Disorderly sparks fly
Fiery flashes in the night sky.
So loud that the racket
Becomes a low dull dense hum
Ascending upwards

And then landing like dynamite
The crackers drop.
Rumbling through the silhouetted city,
Calm and still.

The smoky air settles over the
Illuminated Vatican
Glowing, highlighted rocks observe
As the display crackles out
And the dark closes in.

Ruth H Siller (15)
George Heriot's School

MY WATCHING PLACE

I looked out from my watching place:
Quiet, calm, still.
The mist around me
Flowing and ebbing like a
Silent tide, swamping the
Green pastures underneath with its
Monstrous density,
Never to retreat.

A castle appears on the horizon, where
She once lived. The white-gowned figure
Replaced only by darkness. The crags of
Hidden mountains shepherd the
Few trees which they can hold;
Islands in this wilderness
But still the country of the living.

The fog creeps higher, denser:
The trees disappear -
Gone forever.
I know I need to lift this
Dark veil to succeed;
But I can't.

Philip Williams (15)
George Heriot's School

CLIFFS AT ETRETAT AFTER THE STORM

The wind breathes gently
Rocking and swaying
The boats on the shore.
Clouds of soft pink drift lazily overhead.
Hazy sunshine warms
Golden sand
And
Seagulls cry distantly
The once violent sea is
Calmer now.
Waves of turquoise,
Violet,
Aquamarine.
Rugged cliffs, rise
From the frothy water.
Standing in dramatic
Isolation.
Concealing doors, mysterious caves,
Secret holes and hidden passages.
The air is fresh and crisp.
Haunting music comes from the ocean,
Harmless and quiet
Like laughter after tears or
Innocence after guilt,
The stillness came after the storm.

Fiona MacCuish (15)
George Heriot's School

THE CHURCH AT AUVERS

Dark and twisted. Harsh and pained.
Dominating the landscape and clouding the good,
Obliterating my life force, my esteem not sustained
by the hideous Church which for my mind is food.

Food, food, dastardly food,
Eating away at my soul.
Hides the beauty of the wood
and weakens the vulnerable foal.

Twisted and bitter. Never for the righteous,
A Church full of ill
and of sinful lust,
Casting its shadow on the girl from the mill.

Aah . . . to end it.
My life would pass with ease,
To escape this devilish pit.
My gracious God I must appease.

Alistair Scott (15)
George Heriot's School

SNOW

Snow is falling and falling hard, oh why is it so fast?
But a few weeds and stubble are showing us their last.
The ground is now covered smooth, in soft, sparkling snow,
It even halts the running rivers that used to always flow.
It creates those ghastly daggers hanging from house roofs,
Then it covers many trees making them look like radish roots.
It breaks the silence of the night when tapping windowpanes,
Creating patterns on the windows is one of its favourite games.

Vivienne Li (14)
George Heriot's School

Rock Star

When night has come, and gone the day
I fall asleep and drift away
Into a world, a world unknown,
A secret world I call my own . . .

Chaotic people all around,
Plastic cups carpet the ground,
Heat is rising throughout the place,
The sweat is dripping down my face.

Then suddenly the band appear,
People scream and start to cheer,
I'm there again amongst the crowd,
The drums are pounding, music loud.

There's smoke that's swallowing up the air,
And strobe lights flashing everywhere,
And there he stands upon the stage,
I watch him closely as he plays.

My heart rate rises, I start to shout,
Out of control I then reach out
With open arms towards the stage . . .
Then instantly the image fades.

Despair starts sweeping over me,
Though conscious now of what I see
He still remains there, standing tall,
Smiling sweetly from my wall.

Laura Good (16)
George Heriot's School

Rain, Steam and Speed (After Turner)

Black. Smoke pouring from its funnel.
Thundering like a bull.
Fast and long,
Just as strong
As a thousand horses.
Voices screaming
From its coal-fired engine;
Souls are dreaming.

The noise is inspiring.
Like one hundred drums or more.
Drumming a rhythm into my mind. So powerful
It will stay with me forever.
So powerful, this rhythm has
Inspiring pace, *but* -

A brand new face is soon to come.
So I guess
All will change.
No steam - just dirty diesel,
But still this memory on my easel.
I will remember you.
And when I do
Your rhythm will come to mind.

James Corcoran (14)
George Heriot's School

THE EVOCATION OF THE BUTTERFLIES

Illuminated in the orange glow,
Free spirits flutter high
Cooling the humid day,
To illustrate beauty

Gracefully abstract,
Outlined in the sky,
Their nature hypnotises
Any witness to their display.

In the warm light,
Dancing a complex routine
That others cannot fathom.

Delicate angels of peace,
Being summoned to heaven
In dainty rainbow robes
Of unique appearance,
Bringing the message of sorrow, calm:
Dulling the chaos every day upturns,
With their majestic presence.

Each awoken by the fiery light,
Highlighted in the air:
The time will come, for
The butterflies to ebb and die.

Katharine Fox (15)
George Heriot's School

THE CIRCUS

'Ladies and gentlemen, children galore,
Prepare for a show never seen before . . .
Buy your candy and ice-cream here
It's only a clown, no need for a tear.'

When you are seated, comfy and warm,
Clowns appear, every colour and form.
Their capers are funny . . . your sides will split,
And on comes the star, fully lit.

As she bends, smooth as a snake,
A tightrope walker balances, what a chance to take!
The gymnasts fly like birds in the air,
For many, the thrills are better than the fair.

The show finishes, how short it did seem,
Each character passed, with each, his own theme.
You reach home, too excited to sleep,
The experience was too great for one to keep.

But as you drift, into a dream,
You're there once again with your strawberries and cream.
But no, it's different, you're looking down,
For you're flying like a bird, silly as a clown.

Naomi Maxwell (13)
George Heriot's School

A MIDNIGHT DREAM

The sun grows lower in the sky
A red, hazy mist settles on the horizon
The shadows grow long
Light turns to dark
Day fades to night.

From pale blue, spotted with fluffy, white, cotton wool clouds
To a navy velvet cloak sprinkled with tiny diamonds.

A large golden bead rises
And returns, faint shadows
Trying to mimic sunlight at midday
And travellers gaze in awe
Imagining the planets and galaxies above.

In the distance an owl hoots like a signal for something to begin
And a shooting star flies with the delicacy of a sequin.

And then subtly
With the elegance with which it came
The night is gone once more
Damp crystal dewdrops settle
Waiting for the sun to rise into view.

Jane B M Crawford (12)
George Heriot's School

TRAPPED

Nothing is normal,
everything's bleak.

Nobody cares
they don't even speak.

You want to laugh,
you want to cry.

There's feelings of tension
you wish you could fly.

Gone are rich meadows
streaked with flowers.

There's no one to love
everyone cowers.

You feel like you're choking
you want to be free

But there's nowhere to run,
there's no other place to be.

Anger and hurt, race
through your mind.

Everything's lost, there's
nothing to find.

Siobhan M Ogilvie (13)
George Heriot's School

THE FOUR SEASONS

Glistening through the sky
The stars bring a twinkle to my eye.
Waves simultaneously crash against the bank.
Continually the waves automatically sank.
Animals bathed on a hot summer's night
Beneath the trees all out of sight.

As the morning drew closer, as the light shone through
Like opening curtains the fresh air blew.
The birds sang, repeating their song and dance
Complete with an all-familiar bird stance.
Soft winds blow through the roofs of the trees,
And out dropped the autumn-coloured leaves.

As the white snow falls and settles
Like a white carpet of snowdrop petals,
Children scream and play together again
Building snowmen with the snow which had lain.
For days on end the atmosphere was cheerful
Until Christmas was over and then again it was peaceful.

Silence is broken as the first bud is seen.
Gradually others started to grow where others had been.
The robin's red breast glows in the early morning sun.
Young lambs in the fields have begun to run.
Beyond the clouds the sun pushes through
For another season to begin brand new.

Jackie Ritchie (13)
George Heriot's School

BONNIE SCOTLAND

Up on the hill I stand,
The cold air blowing in
my face and in and
out of glens.
I hear a faint whisper
in the air.
It's the wind covering
and engulfing everything.

The dull driech day rules
over the land,
It's a permanent headache
and an overcast nightmare.
The dull grey sky is hiding
the barren and heathery
land's true beauty.

The crashing of the waves
is heard along with the
whispering wind.
As the waves pound
against the rocks there's
a real sense of power.

The sparse bare trees
stand tall with nothing to show.
They stand lonely in and
around the heather of
        Bonnie Scotland.

Paul McNally (14)
George Heriot's School

THE FESTIVAL

The festival is here
People have come from far and near.
They come to see the plays and shows
Which are superb as everyone knows.

Along Princes Street the cavalcade goes
With actors and actresses performing their shows.
People have crowded all the pavements
To get a good view of all the entertainment.

The esplanade is getting ready
The flow of people strong and steady.
Up to the castle everyone goes
To one of the festival's finest shows.

The festival draws to an end
The firework display is the final event.
The castle rock becomes alight
It really is a special night.

Nicholas I Johnston (14)
George Heriot's School

SNOW

White, white, all around,
Like a blanket, it covers the ground,
No trees, no grass, no rock can be seen,
As if nothing had ever been.
So quiet, so peaceful, only one sound,
The sound of snowflakes falling to the ground.

Amie Barr (13)
George Heriot's School

THE TIGER

The fearless tiger walks around,
With sharp teeth gleaming,
He wanders through the long dead grass.

He lies low, ready to jump,
His green piercing eyes fixed on every move,
He pounces with great speed,
On the surprised zebra.

The zebra struggles but can't escape,
Defeated by the effortless tiger,
It squeals, it shouts, it tries to run,
But then the tiger bites.

Graeme Hawkins (14)
George Heriot's School

IBROX

Walking along the road to *Ibrox*
Many players I do meet, past and present.
In the ground the crowd does roar.
Out comes the team,
The only team worth watching.
Colin Hendry runs out
Followed by Chasbonate.
Hand-in-hand out comes the captain
With the mascot,
And hand-in-hand they will leave.
Victories!

Richard Mason (14)
George Heriot's School

THE MATCH

The ref blew his whistle to start the game
On came the players and on came the rain.
Iain passed the ball to John
Who in a second was gone
Off down the wing at the speed of light
Which gave Harwick's defenders some fright
John crossed it into the far post
Dave drifted towards the goal like a ghost
Into the corner of the net went the ball
Up jumped the crowd, old men and all
Harwick rocked by this early setback
Tried their utmost to get a goal back
Their efforts though were thwarted by Pete
Who used his hands, his head and his feet
Our team was victorious that day
Maybe they'll go all the way!

Scott Cable (13)
George Heriot's School

SQUIRRELS

Hated, grey autumn thieves,
Many scavenging nuts.
For what do they do to help the world?
Nothing but gather food.

Shy and curious flying among trees,
Fast, swift and agile.
Chased and shot at, they flee in pain,
Climbing and balancing feebly.

Red, evil claws,
Big, bushy tail,
Colourful rodent scampers,
Scurrying into hibernation.

David Jung (14)
George Heriot's School

FLIGHT

I can't tell a lie,
It's easy to fly,
When you know how of course.
The plane's in the air,
The weather is fair,
I think I will join the Air Force.

The first time I flew,
I got a great view,
Of the house that I live in below.
We crossed the Forth,
And headed due north,
Following the flight of the crow.

Now I'm on the way back,
And I'm on the right track,
For a landing at Turnhouse you see.
Line it up quick,
Pull back on the stick,
But the plane wasn't landed by me.

Grant Wilson (14)
George Heriot's School

IMAGINATION

I listen to the whispering waves,
Calling to the gentle breeze,
The birds are soaring high,
Trying to catch the morning sky,
Oh I wish I was there,
To see it all,
But now it's all washed away,
Another time perhaps,
To watch my dreams flow by.

Cara Neish Millar (14)
George Heriot's School

RAT

I am winter, cold and bitter,
I am dirt, homeless and unhygienic.
I am fire, vicious and free,
I am the age in a mansion, old and crumbling.
I am a thief, clever and sly.
My hair is ruffled and brown.
I am a Swiss army knife adapting to my every need.
My teeth unforgiving and worn
I am a trumpet playing sad, sad songs
My voice is squeaky
I am a fur-skin coat
My nose is a hoover that smells only food
I am the world because I am all over the world
I am a *rat* and you can see that!

Christopher Hoban (13)
James Gillespie's High School

DARKNESS

Trains scream as they go past,
The wind howls in the evening.
Railings poke as headlights stare,
Shops grin, welcoming you in.

Cranes spit the leftover rubble,
Skyscrapers, towering above us all.
Trucks growl as they lash past,
Rooftops flinch at the noise below them.

Roads bleed as they're flattened by cars,
Dustbins whisper, quivering with fear.
Vans crawl past carrying their load,
Bricks are laid knowing they're doomed.

Chris Kelly (13)
James Gillespie's High School

HAUNTED CITY

Lamp posts tower, threatening to fall
Sleet stabs everything near
Windows stare, curtains hide
Cars crawl by the slow-moving traffic
Stars whisper at the night below
Telling a story that nobody knows
Ambulances scream past, making people wonder
Old doors slam in the roaring wind.

Rachel Newton (13)
James Gillespie's High School

THE CHOBAN

The Choban's head is as wide as a pumpkin
His arms, like the claws on a fairground machine
The Choban's belly's the waves on the sea.
The great Choban's belly's as round as can be.
The Choban's hair is like a TV,
Shiny and clean and as smooth as can be.

Choban's hands are rough, not beautifully smooth
His hands aren't like lager, a nice silky booze.

The Choban's teeth are white, white as the snow
As for the rest of him, I really don't know.

Paul Connolly (13)
James Gillespie's High School

MY FRIEND

He is like a November night,
Crisp and clear.
His voice is like water
Running over smooth stones
His eyes are like hot coals,
Burning into mine.
His smile is like a tiger's,
Sweet but menacing.
He is like Venus, distant and beautiful.
He is like the sky at night.
He is like a tiger hunting the prey!

Saadia Shad (13)
James Gillespie's High School

SONYA

She's like July, bright and cheerful.
She's like a tuba, playing loud tunes.
She's like a badger with soft black fur.
Like Coke, she is dark and bubbly.
Like thunder she is loud and powerful.
She's like spaghetti, tall and thin.
She's like lunchtime, as she's always hungry.
Like Africa, she's dark but colourful.
Like Saturn, she is mysterious.
Her hair is spiky, like a cactus.
Her smile is angelic, like an angel, but she's not.

Elaine Cunningham (13)
James Gillespie's High School

MY BABY SISTER

She is like summer, bright and happy.
She is like a harp playing peaceful tunes.
She is like a soft white cloud.
Her nose is like a cherry, small and round.
Her eyes are as shiny as two new pennies.
Her hair is as smooth as silk.
She is as cute as a kitten.
She is like Irn-Bru, sweet and bubbly.
She is as cheeky as a monkey
She is like the sun, always cheers you up.
She is as fresh as the air in the countryside.

Katharine Greig (13)
James Gillespie's High School

REBECCA

She is like a little squirrel.
Like the plant Venus, she is calm.
Her hair is like the summer sun.
Like a silver bell, her voice is sweet.
She is like a cool, white lily.
Like faded moss, her eyes are hazel.
Her nails are like a sea snail's shell
Like a floating angel, her walk is light.
She is as pale as a glass of milk.
Like a string of pearls, her teeth gleam.
She is like the fresh month of April.
Like the early morning, she is peaceful.
She is just as delicate as a china doll.

Katie McAra (13)
James Gillespie's High School

ALISON

Alison is like the spring, inquisitive and new.
Like a monkey fooling around,
Or different like Irn-Bru.

Her personality is like twelve noon,
When the day is in full swing.
Unpredictable like a storm but blinding as the sun.

Her teeth are perfect like daisy petals,
Her eyes like crystal balls.
Her hair shines like polished gold,
                        underneath the sun.

Sheryl Balloch (13)
James Gillespie's High School

JENNY

She is like summer, warm and happy,
Like a fiddle playing cheerful songs that never end,
She is like an orang-utan,
With her cheeky smile and mushed-up food.
Like New Zealand, she's small and sunny.
Her eyes, liquorice allsorts, are round and shiny.
Her teeth Polo mints, are white and fresh.
Like chocolate, she's irresistible,
Like an orange, she is sweet and soft.
She is like the warmth, giving everyone a tan,
She's round and bouncy like Mars.
She is like an orangeade drink,
She's orange in colour and fizzes.
She is like a daisy, little and pretty,
Like a teddy, her ears are furry.
Her voice, like a fairground, is high and full of fun,
Her hands are like pancakes, small and flat.
Her smile? Like a rainbow,
Crossing over good and bad.

Fiona Rutherford (13)
James Gillespie's High School

LION

I am fire. Hot and fierce.
I am an Armani coat. Golden, soft and silky.
I am Kenya.
I am summer. Hot and fiery.
I am pineapple juice. Tangy, smooth and tasty.
My voice is thunder roaring loud enough
                              for everyone to hear.
I am a truck. Fast and loud.

Sonya S Mansoor (13)
James Gillespie's High School

BABY

He lies sleeping
Tiny, warm, content
A face of trusting innocence
Small hands curled tight

Does he dream
Of growing strong and sturdy?
Of playing and learning?
Of running and laughing?

I look down and remember
Glimpses of childhood
Freedom of decision
And wish him happiness
And strength.

Neil Watt (14)
Knox Academy

FREYA

Freya is a bouncy girl
Always happy and smiling
Tiny hands and tiny feet
All, always squirming.

She has big brown eyes
And curly hair
Skin as soft as a petal
And when she laughs she makes
        you feel happy and warm.

We take her to the park sometimes
She plays happily on the swings
But when it's time to go
She screws up her face and screams.

She can count to ten
And read a book
She eats by herself
But still likes her bottle at bedtime.

She has two cats called Cousek and Soula
She loves pulling their tails
But when they scratch her she isn't very happy
And hits them on the nose.

Freya is a bouncy girl
Always happy and smiling
Tiny hands and tiny feet
All, always squirming.

Elinor Douse (13)
Knox Academy

LINKSFIELD ACADEMY

The silence is shattered by the first wave of children,
Streaming from all directions,
Towards a large dark foreboding grey building.

Four floors of classrooms,
Teachers sitting at their desks,
Cups of coffee in their hands,
Taking their last breaths of freedom for the day.

The bell has rung,
Registration has begun,
Tick, Tick,
Cross,
'That's Nicola absent. No surprise there.'
'Lorraine?'
'She'll be here in a minute.'
Just another Monday morning.

A few solitary souls are left,
Wandering aimlessly towards the school,
You may wonder why they bother.

Interval has come and gone,
The day is in motion,
The party in full swing,
The first punishment has been given,
How many more are in the wings?

Lunchtime has arrived,
The cafeteria is crammed full,
'Quick, let me look at your homework!'

At last, the bell has rung,
Eventually the evening has begun,
You can almost hear the building breathe a sigh of relief,
As the last teacher quietly drives home.

Ellen Raine Leaver (14)
Knox Academy

THE FAIR

The towering roller-coaster,
The people's cries,
Sally watched with wide startled eyes.
Never before had she seen such sights,
Never before had she had such frights.

Again and again she went on the rides,
Again and again she was filled with surprise.
Life before wasn't like this, she didn't possess a thing.
There was no reason to smile,
No reason to sing,
But now there is happiness and joy,
And she is always given another toy.

Sally is no longer an orphan,
She hasn't been one since autumn.
Now she lives in a warm house,
She is overjoyed as there isn't one
                        single rat or mouse,
She has a family to love her,
And her very own mother.
Life is good now,
But Sally still wonders why and how!

Kirsty Bisset (14)
Knox Academy

THE MASCOT

On Saturdays the mascot is so proud,
For he is to lead out his heroes, in front
                  of the screaming crowd.

Before the game, he speaks to the players,
He can't believe they've answered his prayers.

Just before kick-off, he gets a photo with the team,
And in doing this he fulfils his dream.

When the match eventually begins,
The mascot hopes his team wins.

At the end of the half there is no score,
The mascot thinks the game's a bore.

In the second half, a goal finally came,
This was enough for his team to win the game.

At full-time when his team has won,
The mascot can't wait for the next game to come.

Ross Blair (14)
Knox Academy

TOM

Tom is a tall, blond-haired boy.
He makes his bed in a bale of hay.
He chases the chickens on the farm,
But he never does them any harm.

Farmer Nisbet says he's the bane of his life,
But he is secretly loved by his wife.
Every night she leaves him his dinner,
Even though he is a sinner.

Tom's spirit is wild and free,
He thinks to himself 'They'll never catch me!'
He goes to school to play with the children,
But has to leave when the teachers scold him.

One day he'll find a home,
And hopefully he'll no longer be alone.

Colin Wood (14)
Knox Academy

THE PLAYGROUND

Rosy-cheeked children dance around,
in the small enclosed area named the playground.
They laugh and cry due to pure joy,
pigtailed little girls and handsome little boys.

Skipping, hopscotch, tag and races,
send the children through all their paces.
Full of energy that seems so endless,
they hardly notice the small wheelchair-bound Elspeth.

Elspeth sits and watches with envy,
working herself up into a shallow little frenzy.
Her wheelchair is hard and cold against her T-shirt-covered back,
and her wheelchair is stuck fast in the playground's muddy track.

Then one handsome little boy dances over,
and offers Elspeth a four-leafed clover.
She reaches out her hand and her expressive eyes
shine with tears as she sighs.

Carrie McDonald (13)
Knox Academy

THE BLACK PANTHER

A big black panther is running through a field,
Coming closer and closer,
Every second.
I run and look for somewhere to hide,
Too late,
The beast is at my side.

It growls fiercely and snaps at my hand,
The pain is unbearable as it pierces through my skin,
Its eyes are bright red and look at me like lasers,
Its teeth are bright white and gleam
Like razors.

Suddenly I hear a yelp and a thud,
As the monster falls
to
the
ground!
Carefully I turn around,
I cry in exclamation
When I see the creature lying there,
A transformation.

I quickly run and sit by its side,
Its eyes no longer red and teeth no longer sharp,
I couldn't believe that I could be so wrong,
To find it was my dog Ben all along.

Gillian Welsh (14)
Knox Academy

POETRY

I've to write a poem about anything,
But I can't think what to write.
I've thought and thunk and thunk and thought
And thought and thunk all night.

When it comes to writing poems
I'm afraid I draw a blank.
When the teacher asked for this
I'm afraid my heart just sank.

I've thought right through the morning
And halfway through the day.
And what you see before you
Is all I have to say.

Some day when I've left school
Prime Minister I shall be.
The first law I shall bring in
Will be to outlaw poetry.

I've used up three whole pencils
And used my rubber to the bone.
As the time draws nearer to hand it in
I start to moan and groan.

Thinking about all this poetry
Starts to make me spin.
About this verse I have my doubts
I think I'll pack it in.

Jennifer Caldwell (14)
Knox Academy

THE CLEVER CHILD

George Bright was no ordinary boy,
He was not easily satisfied with a toy.
For his sixth birthday he wanted a calculator,
Unfortunately he got a toy alligator.

All of the other children hated him,
Mainly because he called them dim.
In primary five George was moved to primary six,
This was because he made everyone feel thick.

His first year report was as good as it gets,
He was given an award for his project on pets.
His essay on bees was a task,
But he finished it top of the class.

George dreamt of being a pilot,
But his eyesight would not allow it.
Being forced to change his direction,
He became a chef of perfection.

Now George has become a financial whiz,
This he thinks really is the biz.
With money to spend and problems to solve,
Nothing now could make George dissolve.

Gordon Drummond (14)
Knox Academy

HEAVEN

Riding along
With the golden moon
Shining on my face,
The ground firm
Beneath my horse's hooves,
Is heaven for me

The song of the lark
Brings joy to my ears,
Even the coyote
Howling for food,
Is heaven for me.

Colin Fairgrieve (13)
Knox Academy

WINTER

Winter came surprisingly quickly
Those grey autumn skies
Turned into creamy winter ones.
All too slowly the wet,
Leaf-ridden ground dissipated
Only to be replaced by
A soft light blanket
Of crisp consistent snow.
This layer of pure white
Strangely warms my body.
The cold, fresh air fills
My lungs invigoratingly
As I frolic in this barren new landscape
Which I found one
Christmas morning.
Winter is my favourite season
And always will be.

David Thomson (13)
Knox Academy

CHOICES

We make millions of choices every day,
Nobody's choices are made in the same way.
How do we pick them? How do we choose?
Sometimes we win and sometimes we lose.

Everyone has their ways and their reasons,
It may depend on the time of the season.
It may depend if they're happy or not,
They may even make a choice because they have spots.

Whether to go up or stay on the ground,
Are you afraid of heights or do you love to fly around?
No two minds can think exactly alike,
It's as though your own thoughts are having a fight.

Choosing when to say yes and when to say no,
If you're going to stay or going to go.
I will never understand the making of choices,
Whether it's listening to your heart or other people's voices.

Wendy Rees (13)
Knox Academy

AUTUMN PARK

Autumn is the time for leaves,
Many colours on the trees,
The leaves are red and yellow and brown,
Always floating, sailing down.

Many small children run around,
A tiny crunch as their feet hit the ground.
The chirping of birds can be heard far away,
As people sit on benches admiring the day.

Everyone leaves as day turns to night,
The moon and stars shine on bright.
The chattering of birds raises the sun,
As another day in autumn has just begun.

James Walker (14)
Knox Academy

DRUID'S BOTTOM

Darkness swirling all around me
Evil eyes watching,
Steadily following my every move.
The wind howls like a ferocious wolf,
The ground is moving underneath me,
The tall trees are bending over sideways
with the wind,
And I hear crackling in the distance,
Then getting closer.

I run terrified,
Noises behind, getting closer,
Something brushes my shoulder,
I run my fastest ever,
A shape looms ahead,
Drawing me towards it,
A light.

I rush towards the door,
I fall into it,
Suddenly light is everywhere,
Comfort and warmth surround me,
Safety surrounds me.

Amanda Davidson (13)
Knox Academy

THE SHIP

In comes the ship, a looming giant,
Ready for us to set sail.
It swallows us like a ravenous fox,
And keeps us safe inside.

The chimney smokes like a cigarette,
The smoke getting thicker and thicker,
Everyone rummages around inside her,
Shops scattered here and there.

Suddenly she comes to life,
With a single rumble from her horn.
Everyone cheers, we're ready to go,
As we start to move out slowly.

We turn around and head out of the port,
Everyone watches us go.
Out we move like a creeping lion,
Ready to pounce on its prey.

Inside the party begins,
The ship's belly starts to rumble.
With songs and shows and live entertainment,
The jealous onlookers at the side.

Overnight I happily listen,
To the rumble of the ship moving along.
When we arrive in France in the morning,
I'm sad to get in the car.

She spits us out one by one,
I look back to see her again.
We turn the bend, she disappears,
But remember there's still going home.

Graham Stewart (14)
Knox Academy

ANIMAL CRUELTY

Treating animals badly.
Is not the thing to do,
What is the point in hurting them?
'Cause what have they done to you?

People dump them by the road,
And leave them there to die,
Leave them in an awful state,
Why do they do it, why?

Pets are kept by lots of people,
Who should care for them as well as they could,
But of course there are a few who don't,
Why they have pets, that I've never understood.

It's not just pets that are the victims of cruelty,
There's farm and wild animals too,
Cattle and sheep exported for meat,
And lions cooped up in a zoo.

Cows, sheep and pigs are slaughtered,
But get awful treatment before,
Put into cramped cages with no room to breathe,
This awful torture should happen no more.

Put an end to all the cruelty,
And just think how animals may feel,
'Cause if the same thing happened to you,
I'm sure we'd hate such a raw deal.

Laura Barrack (14)
Knox Academy

DREAMS

The horses groomed and saddled,
Their manes blowing in the fresh wind,
Calmly stand, waiting.
Looking forward to the run ahead.

The sun shines down over the prairie,
As the birds fly high in the sky,
The horses glide through the long green grass,
A shimmer of light flashes in their eyes,
They slow down,
There in front is a beautiful gleaming lake.

The reflection of the sun is orange on the water,
Where a tiny ripple appears from a sparkling fish.

The peaceful breeze rustles the leaves of the trees,
And the long green grass,
The air feels cool and fresh,
We lie down on the soft sweet grass, staring up at the sky,
Our eyes close
We take the world into our dreams.

Naomi Cassells (13)
Knox Academy

CHILDREN

Children are born every day
All special in their own way
Different childhoods, different lives,
All grow up into different guys.

Different problems will come their way
Some will go, and some will stay
One day they'll have children of their own;
But that is another tone.

At the park the children play
On grass, trees and there they stay
Their mothers watch and drink their cup;
And see their children growing up.

Zoe Harris (14)
Knox Academy

WAITING

The girl sits and silently watches the clock,
She waits for each minute to arrive.
There is nothing she can do except wait,
They'll get her no matter what she does.

They wait for her outside the gates,
She's tried to escape but it never works.
There's nothing she can do except face them,
They'll get her no matter what she does.

She doesn't know why they chose her,
One day they'll stop, she tells herself.
There's nothing she can do except hope,
They'll get her no matter what she does.

She hates them but that doesn't help,
They know she hates them but they think it's fun.
There's nothing she can do except hate them,
They'll get her no matter what she does.

At home she says that she is ill,
So she doesn't have to face them at school.
All she can do is wish it would end,
They'll get her no matter what she does.

Eilidh Imrie (14)
Knox Academy

ALONE

All alone on a faraway cay
All my hope is lost
How long will I last
Is this the end for me?

I'm cold, wet and hungry
Wondering what to do,
Should I get aboard the raft,
Or is that the wrong thing to do?

I'm a blind boy with a cat
Sitting on an island
Stew cat sniffing the salt air
Whilst I am in despair.

He's totally unaware of the situation we face,
The all-seeing, knowing cat is content to wait
But my heart races, my senses heightening
Waiting, listening, feeling,
But unseeing what lies ahead.

Daniel Brunton (12)
Knox Academy

PEACE AND QUIET!

The guns are firing and the soldiers moaning,
Far from the birds singing and the cattle roaming,
How I long for the distant sigh
Of fast river, flowing by.
The silence of the hills,
Is like time standing still,
But all that is far from here.

The trench is muddy and the smell cruel,
We don't sleep and our bellies are never full,
The rats and lice run free,
If I could that's how I would be,
Not cramped in this trench,
Waiting for death to claim my soul!

Ben Henderson (14)
Knox Academy

SILENCE

The freedom of the prairie,
Wind blowing in the horses' manes.
Sun shining down on the world
beneath us.

The speed increases
The world flies by
We two alone
Separate from the world.

The prairie vanishes,
The ground eclipsed by the trees.
The lake appears
Sun glistening on the waters
Like the smooth glass on a mirror.

Everything is silent.
As in the dead of the night,
Except for a soft breeze whistling
through the trees.
The world has stopped.

Fiona Ross (12)
Knox Academy

Running Away

On my beloved horse again
The fresh wind racing past my skin
On that bright and breezy day

Together again
But anxious feelings filling my head
As I gallop through
The bright, sweet-smelling yellow field
Where the smell of pollen
Combs my nostrils

I cling like a leech to her mare
My horse - so alive like a real
Rodeo horse.

I hear her steady rhythms,
One, two, one, two, one, two,
So exciting
I never want it to end
I have rescued my rodeo horse.

Fiona McGillivray (13)
Knox Academy

War

The whoosh of the engine in a World War fighter,
The crack of rifles gunning down a poor blighter.
The drone of the engine overhead,
The crying of people as they die in their bed.

Two giant armies in a deadly fight,
Thousands of soldiers dying every night.
Hundreds of tanks trundling over the lands,
Carefully planned landings on the Normandy sands.

Battleships trawling for enemy merchant ships,
On a U-boat sonar they show up as blips.
Depth charges dropped to flush out the monstrous craft,
Blood-soaked survivors float out on a handmade raft.

Pushing on to Berlin, the enemy's on the run,
Some don't quite make it and are killed by a gun.
The Nazis have been defeated after a long war,
Now everyone will party as there's peace forever more.

Simon Mackie (14)
Knox Academy

PEACE

The wind, warm and lazy,
Brushed past my face
Like a soft blanket.
The sun beamed down
From the shimmering sky.
Coloured flowers
Like an artist's paint pallet
Brightened the way.
The grass
Was an ocean of rippling waves
When the wind blew.
The sweet smell of flowers
Drifted in the warm breeze
Like honey from the bees.
The crickets chirped
And the birds sang
In the peaceful silence.

Michelle Murray (13)
Knox Academy

JOHNNY

When Johnny goes exploring,
he might take his motor car,
to travel all the way to India
which is rather far.

When Johnny goes exploring,
he might need his ship to sail,
and take with him his sword and patch,
fight pirates and go on a treasure trail.

When Johnny goes exploring,
he might take his horse to ride,
and he'll take his gun and holster
and fight cowboys for the sake of his pride.

When Johnny goes exploring,
his sister might go,
but she might tell her girlie friends,
and then everyone would know.

When Johnny goes exploring,
perhaps he might take his friend, Ross,
but he's not brave and cannot hunt
and that would only make Johnny cross.

When Johnny is finished exploring,
he'll wake up in a cosy bed,
and look around his familiar room
and realise it's all been a dream in his head.

Bernadette Quinn (14)
Knox Academy

PEACE

I lie low in the trenches with my gun by my side
Next to me lie men, bleeding on the ground
I think of their wives and children back home
And know they long for peace.

Tears roll down my wounded face
Washing away the blood
I cover my ears and close my eyes
And wish this nightmare would end.

I hear screams and pleas from far, far away
And I feel for the souls of those like me
Of those in pain and those in need
And know they too long for peace.

Sara Jalicy (14)
Knox Academy

ALONE

I feel like a fish without water,
as I sit beside Stew cat.
I can hear the waves clashing against
each other.

As I lie down, the tears flow,
I feel the pain and hurt inside.
Blindly try to find my way,
But it's so very hard.

I'm worried that no one will save
me.
I try hard not to think about it,
I feel isolated and alone.

Lisa Douglas (12)
Knox Academy

MY BEST FRIEND

I got him when he was only six weeks old
He was small, cute and coloured gold
He always behaved and was never bad
It was the best present I'd ever got from my dad
I played with him and took him for walks
The only thing wrong was that he couldn't talk
I call him Slim as he was in good shape
I fed him snacks, mainly grapes
When I was out all the neighbours played with him
They all liked him my dog Slim

Then one day when he was nearly ten
I got out of bed and went to his den
Where had he gone, where could he be?
He used to always stay beside me
I checked in the garden, then went to my dad
I knew something was wrong as he looked sad
He started to speak and put his hand on my head
'I'm sorry son but Slim is dead'
I ran to my room and started to cry
Why did Slim have to die?
It was like a bad dream that would never end
He was definitely my best friend.

Ian Ross (15)
Knox Academy

WAR

The sounds of war -
The air raid sirens howl,
Through the night sky,
In the cold dark shelters,
Children shake and cry,
As the world reverberates above them.

The sights of war -
Men, women and children,
Lie on the ground,
Their bones and blood scattered,
While their families grieve,
For their loved ones who mattered,
Tears roll down a small girl's face.

Jessica Laycock (13)
Knox Academy

WINTER DREAMS

The wind
Rushed through the trees
Like whips on a bare back.
The moon shone in the icy blue sky.

The grass
Flickered like flames
Dancing in a fire.
The stars in the cold night sky
Shone like lights
Lighting the world.

My horse
As white as snow,
Lay next to me.
I listened to her soft breathing
In the silence of the cold night air.

Emma Booth (13)
Knox Academy

ESCAPE

The time has come.
We are shadows in the still night,
Stealthily creeping through the leafy trees.
Ever listening, ever stumbling,
Ever wishing to be free.

Slimy swamp water oozes between our toes.
Crocks and turtles - who knows what lurks below?
The smell and sound of danger makes us cautious,
As we follow the one who says,
'I can help you to escape.'

Nothing can deter us
As we follow the raging river,
Water crashing in our ears.
We are weary.

We creep along - quiet as mice.
In the distance we can hear
The hounds baying, drawing closer,
With each step and every breath.

We are safe now -
Past the river and concealed in a hedge.
Someone will soon come
To take us away to a place
Where we can be free.

Freedom.
A wonderful word;
A word that brings happiness,
A wonderful privilege.
A place where we
Need no longer be slaves.

Natalie Rolph (13)
Knox Academy

LEAVING

I'm going to cry now
It's too sad
Maybe he's going to die
My brother, my baby, eighteen years.

If I close my eyes I will cry
Someone who has not yet lived
Someone who may never fulfil his ambitions.

He's just a child
Standing before me
But he has grown too old already
What if he doesn't come back
A pain in my throat . . .
There are no words.

I don't want him to see my tears . . .
He's my baby brother
He has to go -
War is calling.

The hug is not long enough
The tears fall
I long to have time back to fill more fully
Greedy to relive all our memories.

The train whistle blows and he is gone.

Alice Miles (13)
Knox Academy

GUILT

I'm back, I've survived.
But underneath I know I've killed many men,
I haven't told Ma that I've killed in the war,
I haven't even told Pop.
But I feel they know, somehow,
That I didn't have a choice.

Back when I signed up,
I felt OK about the war.
I never thought about the gore,
When we were in the trenches, it was very loud,
I saw things I didn't want to see.

But now I'm home,
I feel guilt.
I have taken away someone's life,
I have taken away someone's life.
The words go round and around,
I feel sick.

Just think of some German mum,
Sitting alone by the fire.
Reading the telegram,
Tears spring to her eyes.
'We are sorry to inform you that your son has died,
Doing his duty for our country.'

I've done my duty,
And I survived.
But somehow I've not,
Somehow I have died.
I have died in my mind,
In my mind.

Calum Champion (13)
Knox Academy

AIR RAID!

The night was silent, silent and still,
Anticipation hung in the air,
As the pilots waited, waited with baited breath,
For the signal that might not come.

The silence was pierced with a rat-a-tat-tat,
As the Morse code receiver burst into life.
The pilots rose with an air of indifference,
Wished each other luck, and climbed in their planes.

Twenty planes left England, flying low over France,
Into Germany, where they were greeted with chaos.
Flak flying around, hitting the wings,
Hoping that they wouldn't be hit down.

A plane to the right was hit,
The crew parachuted to the ground.
Hopefully they were alive,
Hopefully they were safe.

Bomb! The signal from the radio repeated,
The crew bombed the town below.
Back though the search lights and the flak, they flew,
Back to the safety of England.

At the airfield the ladies waited,
The mothers, daughters, wives waited,
Waited for news of their loved ones,
But only seventeen planes returned.

Kerry Macpherson (14)
Knox Academy

WAITING

The day he left,
I was silent.
For days, nights,
I was silent.
I sat at home thinking of
My father.

I remembered the days we had together,
Laughing and joking.
I miss them and I miss
My father.

When the doorbell or telephone rang,
I would rush only to be disappointed.
I longed for the day he would
Stride into the house,
And pick me up in his strong arms.

My mother is hurting and longing
She doesn't say.
But I understand.

The war is over.
We have won.
And I am still waiting.
The doorbell rang and I knew.
He was never coming back.
The war has taken my father,
Forever.

Laura McDougal (14)
Knox Academy

THOUGHTS OF HOME

I feel alone.
However, I am surrounded by men.
So lonely,
As in my mind I see my wife smiling,
And my children playing in the yard.
Will I ever see them again?

I try,
Not to think of the lies I was told,
Of all the medals and heroism.
Instead,
I remember the good times.
Or I try.

What would I give to return home?
To live in safety and not fear.
I don't understand.
The people we are killing are just like us.

I sit.
And look up at the black sky.
It suffocates me.
The night air smells like fumes,
I find it hard to breathe.

Joanne Woodhead (14)
Knox Academy

THE EMPTY STREET

Shadows lurking in the empty street
Made me wonder
What was lying beyond my window?

Shimmering shadows in the silent street
Shining through the curtains
Created weird shapes.

There were no sounds, but somehow it felt
As if everyone was standing together,
Laughing at me through that window.

But then I discovered there was nothing to fear,
There was no need to shed a tear;
It was all a figment of my imagination.

Stephen Elcock (15)
Knox Academy

HIS IMAGINARY FRIEND

I remember the delightful squeals and giggles
Of my little brother
Filled the whole room
Like a sweet fragrant flower
I watched as his imagination wove a spell
Turning an empty space into a lifelike person

Now I see him laughing with his friends outside
And I realise our childhoods
Are slipping away
Like the sands of time
It will never be the same
And there is nothing I can do.

Alison Stalker (15)
Knox Academy

CHRISTMAS EVE

Outside the snow fell thick and fast,
Inside the tree's lights glowed.
And I lay tucked up in my bed
Excitement beginning to grow.

Hundreds of thoughts filled my head,
Of Santa and his sleigh.
With his big red coat and fluffy beard,
Travelling on his way.

Rudolph and the others,
Flying through the sky.
It really must be magic,
That made those reindeers fly.

My thoughts were interrupted,
By a noise outside the door.
'It must be Santa come at last,'
Excitement growing more.

The bedroom door opened slowly,
A figure crept in, quiet as could be,
I slowly opened my eyes,
As curiosity got the better of me.

But the sight I saw before me,
Made me feel upset and sad.
For the figure wasn't Santa Claus,
It was only just my dad.

Louise Dickson (15)
Knox Academy

WINTER

The nights drew in
As the temperatures dropped.
The young boy knew now
That winter was coming.
The snow started to fall
Like pieces of cotton,
And icicles formed
Like clear, pointed daggers.
But best of all the snowmen,
Anywhere and everywhere,
A garden, a pavement
He built them.
Then the joy of smashing them up,
And the snowball fights started.

Then a police car stopped,
And the solemn figures
Looked like huge, dark monsters.
They called him over,
And thoughts started to churn inside.
He hesitated,
His heart beating like a drum,
Took a deep breath and ran over.

He climbed in sobbing
And crying for his mammy
But she was gone now,
Left the world for ever.

As he sat in the station
He couldn't believe
That winter could do
Such a *terrible* thing.
His granny came in
And held him tight,
But he thought now
The joy would never return,
As the nights drew in.

Finn-Erik van Barneveld (15)
Knox Academy

ALONE

I am left alone on a forgotten cay,
There is nobody here as far as I can see
Nobody apart from a cat called Stew
But he will not speak, just miaow and mew
And he can't help me, he's just a lazy cat
He just lounges about on a palm frond mat.
A mat that me and Timothy had sewn
But now I have to make them alone.
Every night I listen for sounds from the sky
But really my hopes aren't high
That I will be rescued or found one day
Will someone save me? I just can't say.
So, here I am on a forgotten cay
No sound to be heard, just the lapping of the sea.

Samantha Robson (12)
Knox Academy

ALONE

When he died
I went and sat there,
I was so sad,
I did not know what to do,
I just held Stew cat.

When I stopped crying,
I got up,
And went to look for food,
I caught a big red fish.

As I ate,
I thanked Timothy
For teaching me independence
As I sat alone on the island.

Christopher Rudyj (11)
Knox Academy

A LION'S PREY

As it creeps and crawls through the forest,
Sniffing here and there,
As animals sense to get ready to run away.
But with a leap then a pounce,
The lion is already there.

Sarah-Louise Wrigley (12)
Knox Academy

HUNTING FOR CONKERS

I remember the conker season,
we all went mad for no apparent reason,
We saw conkers all the time on telly,
from the playschool presenter with the big round belly,
The ground was dotted with little green specks,
And our hands were covered in little red pecks,
For when we touched them, the blood ran red,
Our mums would comfort us, and stroke our heads.
So we learned to use our feet,
and that tough green shell,
was always beat,
to reveal the hidden treasure.
Little balls, shiny and brown,
from the tree they fell,
They were made in heaven,
we could tell.
Big ones, small ones, ones shaped like eggs,
made my sister beg and beg.
And then we holed and strung them,
And then we battled,
Bash, bash, bash
The conkers rattled.

I was the champion, I always won,
But then came the day when my conker got done,
and someone else won.
'No, no, no, it's not fair!' I roared,
I decided not to look at another conker again,
So while everyone else was having fun,
I was bored.

Mark Clement (15)
Knox Academy

A Friend For Life

Her face stood out,
Like a burning, bright star.
Even in my infantile naiveté,
I recognised her shine.

In my head, I had an image,
A perfect plan;
Of how we would share,
Our childhood together.

Our friendship flourished,
Like a beautiful rose,
In its first awakening
To the world.

Our first exposure
To the intimidating land,
Of reality, was shared as,
We stepped into school;
As if entering the gates of heaven,
Like unblemished angels.

As our rose began to grow, still
We, in ourselves, were maturing also.
The toil of growing up, was eased.
By her presence.

As she grew up,
Through the hardships of life,
She was still shining brightly,
She was always there,
Always shining.

Our rose is growing still,
As are we.
Hopefully our rose will yet ripen.

Eilidh Lumsden (15)
Knox Academy

UNTITLED

Not a star in sight,
But the sky remains strangely clear.
The land is peaceful and still.
A glimmer of light flickers far off in the distance
As someone waves a torch across the sky.

Everything is tranquil,
I am without a care,
I take another breath,
Is there anyone there?
Putting the past behind, where it belongs,
Expecting nothing from the future,
Taking each day as it comes,
Drifting away in a blanket of clouds.

A small flicker from distant skies,
The torch is out, the memory remains.

Melissa Llano (14)
Knox Academy

The Monster Under My Bed

I tiptoed quietly over my toys
Trying not to make any noise.
I paused two metres short of my bed,
Launched myself to it and banged my head.
At last I was safe on top of the bed
But I still wondered if it had been fed
Or if it would try and bite my feet
And have a chew on my succulent meat.
Its smell would rise up from the floor
I couldn't take it any more.
I would hear its grunts while it sleeps
From below the bed its green hair seeps.
After a while I close my eyes
And dream of its disgustingly massive size.
But I knew if I made no sound
The monster wouldn't leave the ground.

It's the thing I've dreaded for many years
I could feel my eyes fill with tears.
My evil, horrible mum said
That I had to tidy under my bed.
I hauled out all my stuff
And exclaimed to myself enough is enough!
There wasn't any monster living there
There's no such thing as a monster's lair.
For all these years I did pretend
But now my fantasy has met its end.

Sam Smith (14)
Knox Academy

SATURDAY

It was the end of a night that had lasted forever,
And Katie and Heather went off for a blether;
In the other direction;
Which left me alone on my way back to home,
Where my heart's meant to be but was never.
I cuddled myself to keep from shivering
From the cold that I'd felt all my life.
My mum always said that my heart would stop working
Through lack of heat in my body and I'd function by brain cells alone.
I went up the alley,
I was told it was quicker, but not quicker for me.
The darkness and deepness of the dank eerie way
Reminded me of how I'd felt today.
But little did I know that as soon as I turned,
My body would change and be cold as if burned.
He sneaked up behind me and I didn't see,
As he pushed and thrust and terrified me.
Two hours before I was happy and singing
And now all I felt was the stinging
Of my heart beating out to be free.
It was over in seconds,
But would be with me for years of my life,
No longer worth living.
I sat on my bed comforted by my pillow,
Waiting for flashbacks that'd been coming and going,
Wiping the tears that flowed like a river,
Down cascading falls.
And as I burrowed into my pillow like a lost little bunny,
I realised for the first time I wanted my mummy.

Alison Thompson (14)
Knox Academy

WINTER DAYS

Frosty mornings,
cold beginnings.
A path of ice,
the snow so nice.

The tree, the house
a sheet of white.
The crisp, the crunch,
the snow so bright.

The sky so dark,
so misty, so pale.
The ball of white
like a giant hail.

The fire is glowing,
so orange and red.
The snow is melting.
It's time for bed.

Before I rise,
the flakes I see
are coming down
in front of me.

The fire is out.
A cold wind moans,
and on the windows
ice reforms.

Eilidh Gordon (15)
Knox Academy

HE DIED SO YOUNG

He died so young.
I didn't understand.
We were both tied up
Together in innocence
Like two doves.
He was my best friend,
Then he was gone.

We were always together.
Played with trains.
Never thought of any dangers that may lie ahead.
We were each other's only friend,
And now we're apart.
Where is he now?
He died so young.

Katie Park (15)
Knox Academy

ONCE SHE HAS GONE

Silence
An open door
A brand new scene:
Polished window sills
Blue carpet suddenly visible
Sprawlings of clothes no longer there

Silence
No more orange peelings
Silent reminders of yesterday
No more smells of baby talc
Or the endless vapours of nail varnish
Wafting through the upstairs landing

Silence
No phones ringing
No voices chattering till late
No half smothered giggles as the door opens
The piano has fallen silent
The computer no longer protests at an impossible command

Gone
Only memories left
Until the silence is filled
At the Christmas holidays!

Catriona Howie (13)
North Berwick High School

BUBBLES

As I look at the window,
I wish I could fly,
Up through the clouds and into the sky.

As I float in my bubble
In the breeze,
Twisting and turning at my ease.

As I float in my bubble
I look through the pink clouds
There in the distance is a rainbow town.
The colours are brighter than the Aurora Borealis
There in the middle is a marshmallow palace.

As I float in my bubble,
Over the town,
Going through a rainbow and then sliding down.

As I float in my bubble,
I see a clock,
It starts going tickety tock.
I look at the small dwarf-like people
I remember what was on the steeple.
I wish I could meet them because they look quaint
But I mustn't forget I might be late.

As I float in my bubble,
I look back down.
There I see my rainbow town.
I know that I can't stay,
So I climb out of my bubble and blow it away
I start to fall and I land on my duvet.

Anna Simpson (13)
North Berwick High School

DREAM

Picture yourself
Walking along a bottle river
Leading to the stairs
At the end a lift
Nobody knows to where

Picture yourself
In a gondola in Venice
Floating along on whipped cream
With trees on your finger
That jingle along.

Picture yourself
On a cloud made of candy
Drifting along the yellow brick road
To look, to go,
To find the snow
The snow on the mountain peaks.

Picture yourself
At the end of this dream
To never ever forget
For the dream will end
At the end of this verse
So don't forget to come back.

Claire Foster (12)
North Berwick High School

SPHENISKOS
(Dream for night)

Mechanically walking with rhythmical beat
Tears of frustration, eyes fixed ahead
Pray for the night

Eyes squeezed tightly, grasping at time
Further and further, falling apart
Pray for the night

A dot on the horizon the ice starts to melt
Pools of frustration to silent cries merge
Pray for the night

Vast is the ocean of evaporating dream
Empty minds clasp empty hands
Die for the night.

Jennifer Peyton (15)
North Berwick High School

EYES

Eyes see everything
Except the feelings inside
Unless you look really closely
They can even hide your pride
But if you want
Eyes can say so much
Just the way you look at him
Means more than a touch.

Kirsty Forrester (14)
Penicuik High School

PAYPHONE

I am a little payphone,
all shiny and new,
I've not made many phone calls,
I'm waiting on you!

Fill me up with all your change,
or maybe use a card,
phone up all your friends,
and don't forget your dad!

You can reverse the charges,
or phone up 192,
very soon an operator,
will be speaking to you!

Please treat me with care,
be careful what you do,
I don't want to be vandalised,
because I'm useful to you!

Jennifer Donaldson (12)
Penicuik High School

SCOTTISH FOOTBALL

Everybody has a team
Rangers, Hearts or Aberdeen
Lots of arguments are caused
Because of all the football scores

When it comes to the *World Cup*
The teams all join together
And pick the best players
And send them on together

Ally McCoist and Colin Hendry
What a brilliant team
Help from John Collins
And the rest of the team

Scotland in the World Cup
Didn't go very far
But we knew we wouldn't
That's the way we are.

Dawn Brown (12)
Penicuik High School

YOUR HAIR

Your hair tells the world who you are
Sleek, dark and perfect
Then you'll go far.

Your hair is the life and soul of you
Short, pink and spiky
Is sure to see you through.

Your hair makes you feel good
Straight, long and blonde
It puts you in the right mood, well it could.

Your hair has bad days, your hair has good days
Short, frizzy and dry
But it sure pays.

Your hair, your hair
Long, short or curly
Spiky, frizzy or greasy
Your hair, your hair.

Nicola Stenhouse (14)
Penicuik High School

MOVING HOUSE

The van's all packed up
We're moving away
It's a warm and sunny
Summer's day

Goodbye to my house
Goodbye to my room
Someone's at the door
Boom, boom, boom

It's the moving men
It's time to go
I'll come back and visit
Perhaps? I don't know

Goodbye, see ya later
Au revoir, cheerio
I wish I could stay
But now I've got to go

The drive seems so long
Though it's only down the road
I can't wait to move in
To my brand new abode

Wow! The house is huge
Although my room is quite small
My mum is in the kitchen
My dad is in the hall

Well, I've got to move in
It's not up to me
I don't know how things will end
Sad or happy!

Gillian Faichney (12)
Penicuik High School

THE NEW TEACHER

The new teacher arrived today
He's tall with enormous feet
He shouts even if you whisper
And don't think of moving your seat!

Today he shouted
Quiet!
Too many corrections
You horrible shower!

When the bell rings
He keeps us in
Says 'You're a nightmare'
You belong in the bin.

With his big feet
He stamps across the room
He smells and he's not funny
As he lands me out a punny!

The bell rings for us
to come back in
I shout 'Can I go to the loo?'
Above the din

Half an hour later
The class was asleep
He walks not hits them on the head
                with a ruler,
But there's not a peep!
Wakey wakey up now.

Kelly Dunbar (12)
Penicuik High School

A LION IN THE OVEN

A lion in the oven
A sea lion in the sink
I went to wash my hands
And she gave me a wink.

The lion loves the heat
So the oven's fine for him
I asked him what his name was
And he told me it was Jim.

The sea lion clapped her flippers
And splashed around with glee
She brought out a little teapot
And offered me some tea.

Katie Meehan (13)
Penicuik High School

THE CREATURE

I was walking through the woods
When I saw it!
It was stood there eating something
It was bigger than I had ever imagined

I crept up on it closer and closer
I got right behind it it turned around,
It was hideous
It had huge claws.
It was a . . . ?

Mark Hansen (13)
Penicuik High School

IF I WERE AN ANIMAL

If I were an animal I would be
a koala sitting high in a tree.
All day long I would sit in that tree,
And everyone would watch me
eating a eucalyptus leaf.

If I were an animal I would be
a bouncing kangaroo.
I'd jump up to the sky and down to the sea.
I'd hop around all day
and have people stare at me.

If I were an animal I would be
a beautiful pony
so children could ride on me.
I'd trot around my paddock
and they would laugh and scream,
it would be just like having a dream.

If I were an animal I would be
a big killer whale who lived in the sea.
I would roam around freely
and eat my tea
And make friends with all the little fishes in the sea.

If I were an animal I would be
a huge big lion
so I could roam free.
I'd prowl around at night,
And kill my prey, by giving them a fright.

Kirsty Gallagher (13)
Penicuik High School

THE WARMTH OF NOSES

Noses don't have any clothes
Even if it's snowing
Or even if the icy wind's
Continuously blowing
Why has no one ever thought
To make their nose a little sock?

When it is snowing
And your nose goes red,
People think they're smart
To put a hat upon their head.
Have they never thought to
Put a sock on their nose,
It would make it nice and pink
Just like their warm toes.

Alison Maitland (14)
Penicuik High School

THE ROLLER-COASTER

I saw a roller-coaster,
It was on a poster.
I asked my mum and she said it might be fun.
I asked my dad and he said 'Are you mad?'
So I went on this roller-coaster
That was on this poster.
It kept on going faster and faster
And at last it stopped.
And now I know why it was fun and
why I was mad!

Keran Hussain (12)
Penicuik High School

A Boy Called Stretchbrain

There was a boy called Stretchbrain
Who had a strange big head
His forehead was long and wide
And his lips were bloody red

His eyes were big and gawky
And his hairdo was quite weird
But no matter where he went,
Everybody cheered

Until one day ickle Stretchbrain
Seemed to go quite mad
All of his great admirers
Kept on pestering his dad

Stretchbrain's head began to look
A bit like a balloon
It must have been all the shouting
'Cos now he's on the moon

The pressure was too much for Stretchy
As his head began to burst
But he just kept on swirling up and up
If only he'd thought about it first

So the sad ending of this story
Caused many people pain
So always remember this little lad
The amazing, innocent Stretchbrain.

Lauren Kerr (14)
Penicuik High School

HORSES

H orses are a lot of fun,
O ats they eat, they like the sun.
R unning, jumping, standing still,
S ee you riding up that hill.
E ating hay up in their stall,
S ee them big and see them small.

A ll of them are cute and nice,
R iding them is worth the price.
E xpensive animals but worth it later,

F riendly, joyful, warm as a radiator,
U nusual sometimes but very jumpy,
N ice in canter but sometimes bumpy.

Horses are fun!

Sarah Blake (12)
Penicuik High School

GLASSES

I wear glasses,
Glasses are fun,
I'd love to have four pairs instead of just one.
I can see the world clearly through the lenses
But people don't care when they've got all five senses,
People laugh, people scream, some stare,
But it doesn't bother me, no I don't care.
As long as I can see
How bright the world can be
I stand out from the masses
Looking gorgeous in my glasses.

Leanne Steel (14)
Penicuik High School

I Had A Little

I had a little hamster,
it ate a lot of oats,
when I put it in some water,
I found out that it floats.

I had a little gerbil,
it was so cute and round,
until my baby niece came along,
and bounced it off the ground.

I had a little pony,
it ran around a field,
until one day it got sunburnt,
and then its skin all peeled.

I had a little kangaroo,
I liked to call it Skippi,
I used to keep it in the house,
But then it got too nippi.

I had a little kitten,
it had little fluffy paws,
until one day when we were playing,
I discovered the rascal had claws.

I had a little fishy,
its name was Alana,
I put my finger in the tank,
and discovered it was a piranha.

I've given up on pets,
the cost is far too much,
or maybe it is just because,
I haven't got the touch.

Steffanie McKenna (14)
Penicuik High School

PERFORMER

I am a performer
I dance, act and sing
Every time I'm on the stage you hear a lovely *ting*.
I am a performer
That is what I do
Everyone enjoys it and I hope that you will too.
I am a performer
I love it and it's fun
Every time you hear and see me, out comes the sun.
I am a performer
I've even learnt to rap
But sometimes all this tires me out, I think I'll take a nap.

Deborah Hush (13)
Penicuik High School

THE STAR

A silver dot in the sky,
What is it? It's up so high,
It shines so brightly at night,
It really is a lovely sight.
There are many of them shining so bright,
But you can only see them at night.
They are all so far away,
And they are still there during the day,
They are stars and they look like dots,
And there are lots.

Sarah Haworth (12)
Penicuik High School

Day At High School

Ring of alarm
The yawn of a tired boy
Up he gets to have his breakfast and go to school.
History first
The tired boy gets a nap there.
The bell goes.
Break. He runs outside eating his Mars bar.
He plays football
Runs away when he breaks a window
Teachers and prefect yell at him to come back.
Does he come back?
No.
End of break.
English next
They are writing poems
Oh no.
He writes the poem.
The lunch bell goes
There's the janitor mending the broken window.
He eats his lunch.
Mark calls him over to play football
They team up with some other people and beat the third year.
The lunch bell goes, to class they go.
Design and tech and then the end of the day.
There's Andrew in the sweet shop
Choosing his favourite sweets as usual.
Home he goes
TV on for the rest of the evening and he is in the chair.

Michael Jeffries (13)
Penicuik High School

THE BLACK CAT

Dark and beautiful like the midnight sky,
The black cat gives a high-pitched cry.
Its green eyes sparkle like a great lagoon,
And its claws try to scratch at the silvery moon.

Its soft black paws pad along the ground,
They're as smooth as silk and don't make a sound.

Its graceful tail is long and thick,
As she walks along it gives a flick.
Her long legs are built for running fast,
If she was in a race she would never be last.

In the forest the snow is lying thickly,
The cat stops to have a taste quickly.

I wonder where this cat is going,
All the time it is heavily snowing.
At last she sees a ray of light,
She is out of the darkness, away from the night.

Finally she emerges from the trees,
She has had a long day and flops down on her knees.

Sarah Wiltshire (12)
Penicuik High School

THE STARS

The stars at night, oh what a sight.
To see them shining oh so bright!
The stars go on, on and on
Just like mowing my back lawn.

Do you like the stars?
I love the stars,
Floating everywhere even around Mars,
How many are there?
They must be everywhere.

Kristofer Buchanan (12)
Penicuik High School

STARS

I was out one night
And saw the stars shining so bright
There were lots and lots
Just like little dots
Spread all over the sky.

There are lots of constellations
Like Leo the lion and Taurus the bull
With all of the rest the sky will be full
But it is just lots and lots of little stars
Spread all over the sky.

All of these stars cover the sky
Some of them even fly
Millions and billions of them
All with bright lights around the hem
Spread all over the sky.

All over the world there are stars
Sometimes you can even see Mars
All they are are fiery balls
Spread all over the sky.

Louise Paterson (12)
Penicuik High School

THE POEM OF KC THE HORSE

This is my horse
He's called KC

People say he
Looks lazy

In the stable
On the yard

They say his fat
Is very hard

But I know it's
All pure muscle

He keeps toned up
In all the bustle.

Claire Rudge (14)
Penicuik High School

THE TINY INSECT

Way down deep in the jungle,
Where the lions roar
and the antelope graze,
a tiny insect lies
curled up and frightened.

Frightened it will stay
for if it walks, or talks, or sings
it surely will be gone
inside a lion's stomach
or in a parrot's beak.

Melissa Edgington (12)
Penicuik High School

SHADOW ASSASSIN

Creeping through the shadow of night.
A glinting blade supplies a little light.
Moving so sleek across the rooftops
a cigarette falls below, he stops.

Scanning the area for sound
he sees his victim and silently drops to the ground.
Proceeding onward to his kill,
the thought of death brings him no icy chill.

He's upon his victim in a flash.
A slice, a scream and a wounded gash.
No one heard or saw the sight.
It happened and finished in the dead of night.

Ross Blaikie (12)
Penicuik High School

HALLOWE'EN

Witches and warlocks,
cats and brooms.

Pumpkins and bats
and a full moon.

Big black cauldrons,
frogs and toads.

Trick or treat, smell my feet,
give me something good to eat.

Craig Gallagher (11)
Penicuik High School

WINTER MONTHS

The days are getting shorter now
The sky is not so blue
Autumn is approaching quickly
And the weather is getting colder too

The leaves on the trees turn red and brown
They look so nice it makes you stare
Eventually though they begin to fall
And the branches are left completely bare

The air gets colder and then comes frost
Soon the fields and trees turn white
As snow gently falls from the sky
Winter has arrived, it's such a lovely sight.

Murray Taylor (11)
Penicuik High School

TWINS

What are you doing for lunch Lauren,
Well for a start I'm Siobhan.
Are you going out tonight Siobhan?
Oh Siobhan's over there, I'm Lauren.
See they have got us mixed up again,
It is such a pain. The OK thing
About being a twin is you can blame
Each other for everything.
The best thing about being a twin is
You are never alone and you're always in company.

Siobhan Baxter (11)
Penicuik High School

HALLOWE'EN POEM!

On the 31st of October
beware,
There are witches and goblins
everywhere.

With pumpkins with faces and
skeletons galore, apple dunkings and
costumes of . . .
Witches, and demons as dark as the night,
if one comes behind you it'll give you a fright!

When it's time to go, you wave goodbye,
and so you wait for next year's ride!

Natalie Lyons (12)
Penicuik High School

WHAT IS THAT?

Is that a mouse on the floor?
Is that a monster at the door?
What is that under my bed?
Oh look over there a creepy head.

Oh no I heard a bark,
Oh why am I afraid of the dark?
Oh Mum please come here,
Oh Mum, Mum a ghost is near.

Mum hide me from a scary ghost,
Oh Mum I hate monsters the most.

Mark Ramage (11)
Penicuik High School